Robert Louis Stevenson
THE TRAVELLING MIND

EILEEN DUNLOP

National
Museums
Scotland

Published in 2008 by
NMS Enterprises Limited – Publishing
a division of NMS Enterprises Limited
National Museums Scotland
Chambers Street
Edinburgh EH1 1JF

ISBN: 978 1 905267 21 7

Publication layout and design by
   NMS Enterprises Limited – Publishing.
Printed and bound in the United Kingdom
   by MPG Books Ltd, Cornwall.

For a full listing of NMS Enterprises Limited – Publishing titles and
related merchandise:

www.nms.ac.uk/books

For John and Mary Robertson

Acknowledgements

I AM GRATEFUL to many people for their help and encouragement in the writing of this book. They have lent me books, given me advice, and kept my work in mind when visiting places associated with Robert Louis Stevenson which I could not reach myself.

I thank the following in particular: Prof. Jim Miller, Margaret Miller, Dr Bob Cowan, David and Anne Baldwin, Kate Blackadder (NMS Enterprises Limited – Publishing), Carol Brodie, Richard Dunlop, Sheila Mackenzie (National Library of Scotland), Hamish and Susan Robertson, John and Mary Robertson, Derek and Irene Smorthit, and the helpful staff of Stirling University Library.

I am fortunate to have Lesley Taylor as my publisher (and editor of this book), and specially wish to acknowledge my husband, Antony Kamm, who has given so generously of his time and expertise to help me. He has solved my many computer problems, compiled the index, and given me the benefit of his encyclopaedic knowledge of manuscript preparation and correction of proofs. As always, I have been sustained by his enthusiasm as well as his practical support.

Eileen Dunlop, 2008

Image Credits

All images and photographs are credited individually on the page. Every attempt has been made to contact copyright-holders for permission to use material in this book. If any source has been inadvertently overlooked, please contact the publisher.

Contents

CHAPTER 1

The Engineer's Child

Poetry cunningly gilds
The life of the Light-Keeper,
Held on high in the blackness
In the burning kernel of night,
The seaman sees and blesses him,
The Poet, deep in a sonnet,
Numbers his inky fingers
Fitly to praise him.
Only we behold him,
Sitting, patient and stolid,
Martyr to a salary.

– 'The Light-keeper', 1869-70 –

THE POET WHO had lighthouses in his blood and deplored the martyrdom of a salary was probably the most famous child ever brought up in Edinburgh; certainly he was the one who recorded his youthful experiences most vividly. Many Scots of an older generation can recall from their own schooldays *A Child's Garden of Verses*, with its gentle, wry evocation of comfortable, middle-class Victorian life, and the picture of a small boy peering from a window at dusk to watch the lamplighter in the street is one of the enduring images of the nineteenth century city.

For we are very lucky, with a lamp before the door,
And leerie stops to light it as he lights so many more. ...

That the street lamps of Edinburgh owed their brilliance to the scientific work of his own great-grandfather, and that he belonged to a family grown wealthy through its obsession with the use of lights at sea, were facts that the child would learn gradually, as he became mature.

Robert Lewis Balfour Stevenson, born 13 November 1850, was the only child of Thomas Stevenson, a civil engineer, and Margaret Isabella Balfour, daughter of a Church of Scotland minister. The boy was named after his two grandfathers: Robert Stevenson, who until 1843 had been Engineer to the Northern Lighthouse Board, and the Rev. Lewis Balfour, minister of Colinton, then a village four and a half miles south-west of the city. Lewis Balfour was present at the child's baptism on 13 December, having stated grandly that he had not 'the smallest objection' to the choice of name. Robert Stevenson, who had been in decline since the death of his wife in 1846, had died four months before his grandson was born. There has been much discussion as to why the name 'Lewis' was subsequently changed to 'Louis', some critics accusing the writer of affectation in preferring the French form. It seems, however, that after the death of his father-in-law in 1860, Thomas Stevenson himself changed his son's name, allegedly because there was a man called Lewis in Edinburgh of whose radical politics he, as a Tory, deeply disapproved. The child was called 'Louis' at home and by his friends, but the Scots pronunciation of his name was apparently unchanged.

In adult life the author of *Kidnapped* and *Catriona* loved to conjure up a dashing, romantic lineage for himself; he claimed both Scandinavian and French ancestry and, imaginatively attached to the Highlands of Scotland, dreamed that he was descended from Rob Roy MacGregor, the colourful outlaw immortalised by Sir Walter Scott. The truth, which he acknowledged more candidly in the later years of his life, was less flamboyant but no less remarkable; and since it contributed as much as fantasy did to his imaginative world, it is worth knowing something of the family into which he was born.

The Stevensons were, unlike most of their class, beneficiaries of the Industrial Revolution which transformed Britain in the late eighteenth and early nineteenth centuries; often among the clever and ambitious in Scotland, a mother loomed large in the success story of her son. Of undistinguished Lowland stock, small shopkeepers until the second half of the eighteenth century, the first Stevensons to do anything at all out of the ordinary were two young brothers, Hugh and Alan, who decided to go into partnership as traders between Glasgow and the sugar plantations of the West Indies. It was an ill-fated venture as both men died abroad of a tropical fever while still in their twenties, but it was the Stevensons' first encounter with adventure, travel and the sea. The younger brother, Alan, left behind in Glasgow a 23-year-old widow, born Jean Lillie, and a two-year-old son, Robert. It was this child who first made the name of Stevenson famous, and he had the love of his mother as well as his own genius to thank for it.

Fortunately for Robert, born in 1772, Jean Stevenson was a strong-minded young woman who believed in education. Although left close to destitution by the deaths of her husband and her father in the same month, she was determined to give her son a good start in life. With a small allowance from her own mother, within four years of Alan's death she had moved to Edinburgh, where she herself had been educated. She could not afford to send Robert to the High School, but managed to secure him a free place at another, and by scrimping and saving paid for him to have extra tuition in Latin and Greek. Jean, like many devout Scottish mothers, probably hoped that her only son would become a Presbyterian minister; a clergyman's high status in the community, as well as the benefit of free housing, made a career in the church an attractive option at that time.

Unfortunately Robert disappointed Jean; he was neither a classicist nor a theologian and, at this stage in his life, not much of a student either. He was still wrestling reluctantly with Greek grammar and elementary divinity when, in 1787, his mother made a pragmatic but highly advantageous marriage with one Thomas Smith, whom she had met at church. Robert acquired a stepfather who had already been twice widowed and was the father of three sons and two daughters.

Originally from Dundee, and like Robert bereft of his father in childhood, Jean Stevenson's new husband was a clever man who had worked hard and was now master of many trades, as an ironmonger, dealer in grates, lamps and oils, ship-owner and underwriter. By the late 1780s, however, his chief interest was in the improvement of street lighting, for which the recent building of Edinburgh's fine New Town provided a golden opportunity. A natural next step was to consider the illumination of lighthouses – until that time a primitive and chancy business. Smith's innovations in this field led to his appointment as first engineer of the Board of Northern Lighthouses, and through him Robert Stevenson found his vocation. Latin and Greek were gladly shelved in favour of mechanics and by 1790, at the age of 18, the boy was formally employed as his stepfather's apprentice and prospective partner. How highly Thomas Smith valued Robert's potential is proved by his giving the apprenticeship to a stepson rather than to his own eldest son, James.

Thomas's generosity was of a practical kind. During the early 1790s he paid for Robert to study civil engineering at Glasgow University, where he was taught by Professor James Anderson, nicknamed 'Jolly Jack Phosphorous', who was said to have suggested the potential of steam power to an adolescent James Watt. Anderson spotted Robert's ability and marked him too as a man of the future. He also instilled in his adoring pupil a belated passion for the benefits of academic study – a conversion that would prove a mixed blessing to Robert's own sons.

In 1796, on his proud stepfather's recommendation, Robert succeeded Thomas Smith as Engineer to the Lighthouse Board, and three years later the alliance of Smiths and Stevensons was cemented still further by his marriage to Thomas's daughter Jean. Such a pairing of stepchildren was unusual even then, and certainly seemed *outré* to the couple's grandson Robert Louis: 'The marriage of a man of 27 and a girl of 20,' he wrote sniffily in *Records of a Family of Engineers*, 'who had lived for twelve years as brother and sister, is difficult to conceive.' It is certainly difficult to conceive of it as a great romance, but perhaps both bride and groom saw the advantages. Just as probably, it was the former Jean Stevenson's way of ensuring that her son inherited the lion's share of Thomas Smith's considerable fortune.

Robert Stevenson held the position of Engineer to the Northern Lighthouse Board for 47 years. The Board controlled the financing of his operations, while his job was to plan and build the lighthouses, frequently in the most isolated, inhospitable and dangerous locations in the country. His achievements and frustrations are well documented elsewhere; here it is enough to say that he built 27 lighthouses, using his own invention of intermittent or flashing lights, while acting as consultant engineer for the construction of roads, harbours, bridges, and, as the Industrial Revolution gathered pace in the early nineteenth century, canals and railways. At home in Edinburgh during the winter, when outdoor work had to be abandoned, Robert took time out from planning and calculating to write an *Account of the Bell Rock Lighthouse Including the Details of the Erection and Peculiar Structure of that Edifice* – not for literary fame, but because he recognised that the completion of this task, in the face of the overwhelming force of wind and tide twelve miles from Scotland's east coast, would stand as his greatest achievement. His energy and commitment were colossal. Honours and gold medals were bestowed on him far beyond his native Scotland, and his position as a man of importance at home was crowned when, in 1810, he was accompanied on his annual tour of lighthouse inspection by Walter Scott. The famous author added his seal of approval to the Bell Rock project, remarking fulsomely that 'no description can give the idea of this slight, solitary round tower, trembling amid the billows ...'. Invited to sign the visitors' book, Scott went further, adding a verse in his own hand:

> *Far on the bosom of the deep,*
> *O'er these wild shelves my watch I keep:*
> *A ruddy gem of changeful light,*
> *Bound on the dusky brow of night.*
> *The seaman bids my lustre hail,*
> *And scorns to strike his timorous sail.*

It was like a royal seal of approval, and Robert's pleasure was immense.

At this stage of his career the 48-year-old engineer could well have afforded to retire and spend the rest of his days as a leisured and well-respected Edinburgh citizen, but that was not his way. The Presbyterian work ethic of his mother and stepfather was ingrained in him, and he continued to spend his summers travelling the roads and sailing round the bleak Scottish coast, supervising construction, solving on-site problems, cajoling and sometimes threatening the men who toiled in constant danger to make his dreams come true.

Winters were passed at his Edinburgh residence, 1 Baxter's Place. This was a house perhaps more comfortable physically than emotionally since, over a period of 22 years, Robert's stepsister-wife had given birth to 13 children of whom only five, a girl and four boys, survived beyond early childhood. Family life must have been darkened by maternal grief and intense anxiety for the welfare of the children who did survive. Robert must often have been glad to escape to his office, where he designed, planned and dealt with correspondence, mostly with his employers, the Trustees of the Lighthouse Board. Robert confessed that he found writing laborious, and his account of the Bell Rock light was long in its gestation. He had little time for literature and when, in his sons' generation, a hesitant literary talent began to emerge, he reacted with bewilderment and dismay. For all his belief in education, his attitude to the training of his four boys was entirely utilitarian. The Latin and Greek they learned at the High School of Edinburgh (where he sent them in fulfilment of his mother's ambition for him and as a mark of his own upward mobility) might, he conceded reluctantly, be read later for occasional entertainment; but it was the study of engineering that had made him the man he was, and the boys can have been left in no doubt that it was to make them too. Three of the sons – Alan, David and Thomas – fulfilled their father's wishes by entering the family business; the fourth, also Robert, whom his father considered a hopeless case academically, eventually studied medicine and became an army surgeon. Despite the interesting dynamic of family relationships, however, only two of Robert's sons are significant in the study of Robert Louis Stevenson – his uncle Alan and Thomas his father.

It was on Alan, the eldest, that the burden of parental expectation fell first and most relentlessly. Alan was a highly intelligent, sensitive young man, with a deep desire to please his father. However, he was not robust, and his childhood frailty was something with which energetic Robert, despite the loss of eight other children, seems to have found hard to sympathise. Equally puzzling to him was Alan's fondness for classics and poetry, and his enjoyment of writing and daydreaming – youthful traits which, as well as poor health, would emerge again in his nephew Robert Louis. It is fair to say that Alan was far too delicate for the harsh outdoor life of a lighthouse engineer, that he was bullied into his profession by his father, and that his tragic example taught his brother Thomas nothing in his dealings with his own son.

Alan's life, nonetheless, was as successful as it was heroic. Suppressing his literary talent and his interest in languages, music and theology, he stoically fulfilled his filial duty. He too was out in all weathers, shivering and soaked to the skin, working in the teeth of the wind and leaving, like his father, one outstanding monument. His was the lighthouse at Skerryvore, a storm-tossed rock twelve miles from Tiree in the Outer Hebrides, which many contemporaries considered an even greater achievement than the Bell Rock light. But although Alan succeeded his father as Engineer to the Northern Lighthouse Board on Robert's resignation in 1842, years of toil and physical stress had completely undermined his health. In 1853 he was forced to retire, aged only 46. He spent the last twelve years of his life fruitlessly wandering round the spa towns of England and France, and living in seclusion at Portobello, Edinburgh, with his wife and children. In these terrible years of pain and depression, religion and poetry were his only consolations. His illness was until recently regarded as primarily psychiatric, but Bella Bathurst, author of *The Lighthouse Stevensons* (1999), makes a convincing case for a diagnosis of multiple sclerosis.

When Alan Stevenson fell by the wayside, the lighthouse engineer-ship was taken up by his two brothers, David (whose son, David Alan, would become the sixth and last Stevenson to hold the position) and Thomas, known as Tom, the youngest of Robert's sons. Writing in a memorial essay of his father in 1887, Robert Louis Stevenson spoke of 'a man of somewhat antique strain; with a blended sternness and softness that was wholly Scottish and at first somewhat bewildering; with a profound essential melancholy of disposition and ... the most humorous geniality in company, shrewd and childish, passionately attached, passionately prejudiced ...'. He went on to mention Tom's failure to master mathematics, his lack of Greek, his love of literature and abstruse theology and his morbid sense of unworthiness – in short a contrariness of character and achievement foreshadowed in his youth at the High School and in his father's house. For years Tom had managed to conceal from his harassed parents the fact that he was doing no school work whatsoever (and being brutally punished by his teachers). By the time he was rumbled there were vast and irreparable holes in his educa-tion, and the displeasure of Robert, a man whose seriousness seems to have lacked any leaven of humour, was as crushing as his disappoint-ment. From then on Tom could do nothing right. His fondness for history and romance was derided, his moral seriousness questioned, and his vacillating over a final career choice the cause of prolonged parental fury. The last straw was Robert's discovery, when riffling furtively through Tom's pockets, of a bundle of papers proving that his youngest son was *actually writing fiction*. His horror was even more acute than on a previous occasion, when he had discovered that Tom had bunked off from a family outing in favour of a solo trip to Portobello.

If Tom aspired to be a writer, however, his ambition was snuffed out by his father as peremptorily as Alan's. At length, exasperated beyond endurance, Robert ordered Tom into the family business where, rather surprisingly, the young man found that the life suited him. He enjoyed the summer travelling which lighthouse supervision entailed, and devel-oped scientific interests, initially in the action of waves and later in optics. He took to a further stage the work on lenses begun by the French physicist Augustin Jean Fresnel (1788-1827) and perfected his father's invention of the revolving light – no doubt fortunate, given his shaky grasp of mathematics, in having a cousin, Professor Peter Guthrie Tait, who could be called on to help with the calculations. Outwardly at least, Tom became a grave and conformist member of Edinburgh society – a

7

Tory in politics, a devout member of the established Church of Scotland, a man of property and increasing substance. Under this conventional carapace, however, there lurked an uneasy and divided personality, at times as determined and stubborn as his father's. Tom was pleasant in company and could be playful, humorous and affectionate in private, but he was also hypochondriac, depressive and morbidly obsessed with his sins. Preparing an address to be read at his own funeral, he tremulously hoped that he would not be 'disowned [by God] when the last trumpet sounds'. During half a century of church attendance, he never accepted the rank of 'elder', due to his sense of his unworthiness even for such a limited elevation from the pew.

*　*　*

Such was the man who, in the autumn of 1847, took a fateful journey from Edinburgh to Glasgow on a railway line opened only five years before. In the same compartment, trundling at no great speed through the flat countryside, were a middle-aged couple and their niece, with whom affable Tom easily fell into conversation. The young woman was Margaret Isabella Balfour, aged 18, whose pleasant, unaffected manner clearly appealed to the 29-year-old engineer. Tom was smitten. Now in a position to support a wife, he hastened to follow up the chance acquaintance, and soon letters signed 'Your affectionate and devoted lover' were arriving at Colinton Manse where Margaret, like Tom the youngest of 13 children, lived with her minister father. A brief engagement followed and, within a year, the parents of Robert Louis Stevenson were married and had moved to 8 Howard Place, on the northern edge of the New Town. Built in the 1820s, this two-storeyed terraced house opposite the Royal Botanic Garden, in a section of what is now Inverleith Row, was among the first in Edinburgh to have a small front garden of its own. The address was not grand, but genteel enough to mark Tom's status as a rising man in Edinburgh society.

If Margaret's family, the Balfours, were no more aristocratic in origin than the Stevensons, they were of somewhat higher rank. Also Lowlanders, they numbered among their ancestors the lairds of Pilrig, a considerable land area between Edinburgh and Leith. Kinship was claimed too with the Calvinist zealot John Balfour, the 'Balfour of Burley' of Walter Scott's *Old Mortality*, who in 1656 assisted in the murder on Magus Moor of the Episcopalian Archbishop Sharp – a

8

notorious incident that would colour vividly the imagination of Margaret's son, clutching as he did at any possible connection with the stirring events of Scotland's past.

More recently, the Balfours had pursued more douce and conventional careers in law, church, medicine and the colonial civil service; a number of Margaret's older siblings had left the manse at Colinton to work in India, where her physician brother John was allegedly the last Briton to leave Delhi when the Indian Mutiny broke out in 1857. Margaret, known to her intimates as 'Maggie', was a handsome rather than a beautiful girl, sweet-natured and blessed with incurable optimism despite a history of ill health. She and Tom were happy together, and a year after their wedding Maggie gave birth for the first and only time. Robert Louis Balfour Stevenson, who had 51 first cousins, was fated to be the sole repository of all his parents' love, hopes, dreams and lifelong anxiety.

CHAPTER 2

The Cummy Years

... For all the story books you read:
For all the pains you comforted:
For all you pitied, all you bore,
In sad and happy days of yore:–
My second Mother, my first Wife,
The angel of my infant life –
From the sick child, now well and old,
Take, nurse, the little book you hold! ...

– 'To Alison Cunningham from her Boy',
Dedication, *A Child's Garden of Verses*, 1885 –

CHILDBIRTH IN THE middle of the nineteenth century was a dangerous business for rich and poor alike. Conditions were unhygienic, instruments unsterilised and there were no effective interventions if something went wrong during labour. Puerperal fever, now known as septicaemia, was a common cause of death in childbirth. The only prescriptions were opium and brandy – more to ease dying than in any hope of recovery. Middle- and upper-class women were better off in that they had more comfortable surroundings and nursing help both for themselves and for their babies, but the risks were common to all social groups. It has been conjectured that Maggie Stevenson had a difficult pregnancy and a hard labour; this has been advanced as a reason why she and Tom, both members of prolific families, had no more children. But it is just as probable that her general ill health and the frailty of her baby were the principal factors in this decision. Throughout their long marriage Tom and Maggie remained a loving and companionable couple – indeed so obviously that even their son, in his 1876 essay 'Virginibus et Puerisque', was moved to remark wryly that 'the children of lovers are orphans'. Yet in the days before reliable contraception, their love-making must have been impaired.

The risks of childbirth were not, of course, only to the mother. Statistics of infant death were by modern standards appalling; even those who survived delivery were beset by dangers unknown in the modern developed world. Babies who could not be breast-fed, either by their mothers or by the 'wet nurses' widely employed by the better-off, were fed bread-and-water pap or, more alarmingly, oatmeal porridge, made in dirty pots, often with dirty water, and administered with contaminated spoons. Such children were at risk of constipation, diarrhoea and longer-term malnutrition. But even for those who survived the hazards of their first months, infectious disease lurked in every corner. Horrifyingly, as late as the 1880s only ten out of every 45 children reached the age of five without having experienced either smallpox, scarlet fever, measles, diphtheria, typhus or enteritis, while deaths from mumps and chickenpox were not uncommon. It is on record that Robert Louis Stevenson had diphtheria when he was ten months old, and as a three-year-old a throat and chest infection so serious that his parents feared he would die if he had a recurrence. No doubt their anxiety was heightened by their own tendency to hypochondria and ill health. For most of little Louis's early years his mother, who had inherited pulmonary weakness from her father and suffered from 'nervous troubles', was frequently confined to bed or to the sofa in the drawing-room. Tom, whose parents had lost five children and whose brother Alan's health deficiency had manifested itself in childhood, fretted constantly about his own well-being as well as that of his wife and son.

Along with health concerns, other anxieties beset the recently married couple. The house at 8 Howard Place, however pleasing superficially, was cramped and dark inside, and so close to the polluted Water of Leith that in warm weather odours of raw sewage and industrial effluent wafted sickeningly through its rooms. In 1853 a decision was taken to move round the corner to larger quarters at 1 Inverleith Terrace, which stood on higher ground and was marginally further from the river. Unfortunately, it was soon apparent that bad had been exchanged for worse; the new house was on a corner, exposed on two sides to the freezing blast of north and east winds. It was draughty and, as its previous occupants could have told the Stevensons, it had damp in its bones. Although its atmosphere was blamed by the over-anxious parents for exacerbating little Louis's frequent head colds and bronchitis, they lived there for more than four years.

Not until 1857 did Tom, with his father dead, Alan retired, and himself installed as a senior partner in the family business, feel secure enough to buy 17 Heriot Row – then, as now, one of the best addresses in the city. This imposing, stone-faced terraced house, with its tall front windows facing south across Queen Street Gardens, provided all the space the family and its retinue required, except perhaps in the matter of sanitation. Throughout the 1860s even such a grand Edinburgh house had no water closet, and its inmates had to make do with chamber pots and a privy in the back garden. Tom and Maggie were home at last, and they would live in the house until Tom died there 30 years later.

Housing was not, however, the only practical problem the young couple encountered at the start of their life together. There were difficulties from the beginning with the nurses hired to look after Louis; before he was 18 months old, two left without warning or explanation, while a third was discovered to have taken the baby into a public house, leaving him bundled up on the counter while she flirted with the customers and imbibed a large quantity of gin. Fortunately the fourth presented a more sober, reliable impression; this was the 30-year-old Alison Cunningham, who came to the Stevensons on the recommendation of Mrs Blaikie of Pilrig Manse, a cousin of Maggie's, whose small son she had looked after for the past four and a half years. Godly, respectable and totally loyal, she was the 'Cummy' made famous by the dedication of *A Child's Garden of Verses*, where she was gushingly described as 'My second Mother, my first Wife'. This fulsome tribute was not accepted without mild protest by Louis's 'first Mother', but she accepted it with her usual good grace.

It is beyond question that Tom and Maggie Stevenson adored their only child. During Louis's sickly childhood it was his father who helped Cummy to nurse him through fractious, sleepless nights; and there is a touching story of how, when the little boy accidentally locked himself in a room, his father knelt at the keyhole to comfort him while a servant ran to fetch a locksmith. Maggie was the proudest and most loving of mothers, recording her son's progress in minute detail, fretting constantly over his health, as is proved by the anxious cataloguing in her diary of his ailments, which included, before he was ten, diphtheria, gastric fever, scarlatina, scarlet fever, whooping cough, bronchitis and asthma. She kept his childish drawings, and helped him to write letters to his father when he was away from home. His father nicknamed him 'Smout', a word meaning the small fry of a salmon, and by extension another small creature. Indeed, there is a photograph of him, aged about three, fair hair curled, garbed in a feathered hat and the kind of girly embroidered coat and skirt made famous by his contemporary, the poets' son Pen Browning. It is the perfect image of a pampered, middle-class Victorian toddler, of the kind that in adulthood probably made its subject wince.

If Tom and Maggie were not 'hands on' parents in the modern sense, it was partly because people of their station in life habitually employed servants to look after their young, and partly because Tom's long professional absences and Maggie's chronic illness made dedicated child care impossible for them. So it was that the nurse was allowed, largely unsupervised, to take over what we would now regard as the parental role, and came to exert an influence over the child that was no doubt well-meaning and kind-hearted but, at least to a modern sensibility, not without a more insidious side.

Alison Cunningham was born on 15 May 1822 in the village of Torryburn in Fife. Her father has been variously described as a fisherman and a weaver; at different seasons he probably practised both trades. Alison grew up handsome and literate enough to read and to keep a diary, though her reading was strictly confined to the Bible, John Bunyan's *The Pilgrim's Progress* and extreme evangelical tracts and diatribes. Reared in the narrowest kind of Calvinism, she was intolerant, stridently anti-Catholic and totally convinced of the rightness of her own views. She was also a professional servant, honest, hard-working and totally loyal to her employers. In the Stevenson household she found both a vocation and a home; she was still living there, an indispensable factotum, long after 'her laddie' had grown up and moved away. Already beyond the age when most of her contemporaries married, it would not be surprising if her frustrated maternal feelings were transferred to little Master Lou.

'She was more patient,' the adult Stevenson recorded in an essay entitled 'Memoirs of Himself', 'than I can suppose of an angel; hours together she would help console me in my paroxysms, and I remember with particular distinctness how she would lift me out of bed and take me, rolled in blankets, to the window, whence I might look forth into the blue night starred with street-lamps and see where the gas still burned in other sickrooms, where also, we told each other, there might be sick little boys and their nurses waiting, like us, for the morning.'

This vignette is brimming with pathos, and it is not the only one; time and again, in sentimental mood, Stevenson paid tribute to the tenderness of 'The angel of my infant life', feeding the legend, by no means displeasing to Cummy, of his nurse as supreme nourisher and comforter. Whether he was trying to deceive his readers, or himself, or anxious simply to put a gloss of normality on a seriously abnormal childhood experience, is hard to say. But Stevenson was far too clear-sighted not to realise that in Cummy he had first encountered the 'divided self' that haunted his adult imagination and inspired one of his most famous books, *Strange Case of Dr Jekyll and Mr Hyde*. She doubt-less had her cuddly moments, but there was also a darker aspect to her personality.

It is not unreasonable to describe Alison Cunningham as a religious maniac, or to say that she made Louis one too. During the wearisome days and feverish nights of illness, she fed his imagination with lurid stories, drawn not only from the beefier parts of the Old Testament but also from the staples of popular Protestant devotion, including *The Pilgrim's Progress* (1678), *Foxe's Book of Martyrs* (1563) and *Memorials of Robert Murray McCheyne* (1844). The first is deservedly a classic, as notable for its sonorous biblical prose as for its dramatic content; the last is a hagiography by one Andrew Bonar of an evangelical Scottish clergyman, who died of typhus in 1843 aged 28, and who probably endeared himself to Cummy by his vocal support of Christian missions to convert the Jews. Neither of these books was pernicious, but *Foxe's Book of Martyrs*, which incredibly was considered as edifying Sunday afternoon reading in Victorian drawing-rooms and kitchens up and down the land, was in a different league altogether. An apocalyptic account by one John Foxe of the torture and burning alive as heretics of Protestants, mostly during the reign of Catholic Queen Mary I of England, the book spared no detail, however harrowing, and recounted with repellent relish the drawn-out sufferings of those condemned to this most barbarous of executions. In most editions the cruelty was enhanced by lurid illus-tration, and it is appalling to think of these horror tales being read at bedtime to a puny, feverish and over-imaginative little boy.

To make things even worse, Cummy had tales to add of her own devising. When not reading 'devotional' works, she was filling Louis's head with accounts of her own Covenanting ancestors, God-fearing seventeenth-century Protestants hiding in the bleak hills not only from their visible enemies but from the spiritual forces of Satan with whom supposedly they were in league. As fearful as the fiend Apollyon in John Bunyan's *Pilgrim's Progress*, this Devil stalked Scotland, 'seeking whom he might devour'. It was small wonder that Louis was afraid of death and suffered from appalling nightmares. As a man of 30, he recalled 'waking up from a dream of hell, clinging to the horizontal bar of my bed with my knees together, my soul shaken, my body convulsed with agony …'. He 'piped and snivelled,' he added, 'over the Bible', and would never speak without adding piously, 'If I am spared'. On stormy nights – not uncommon in Edinburgh – his dreams were haunted by the drumming of horses' hoofs:

> Whenever the moon and stars are set,
>   Whenever the wind is high,
> All night long in the dark and wet
>   A man goes riding by.
> Late in the night when the fires are out,
>   Why does he gallop and gallop about?
>
>   – 'Windy Nights'

Unfortunately, Cummy was not alone in stoking Louis's febrile imagination. Tom Stevenson, who to his credit often sat up through the night with his ailing child, attempted to divert him (frustrated novelist as he was) with tales he had himself invented in the hours between getting into bed and falling asleep. But Tom, as much as Cummy, was obsessed with the Covenanters, and his tales were all of fanatics and martyrs and devilish goings on, with the odd highwayman and pirate thrown in for light relief. Although reputedly at times he alone could soothe the stricken child, it is hard to suppose that his stories were much more helpful in persuading him to sleep than was Cummy's remedy for insomnia – a cup of strong coffee administered at midnight. It is small wonder that Louis waited anxiously for the sound of the country carts rumbling along Heriot Row in the early morning, signalling that the sun was about to rise.

There is no denying the positive influence of Louis's years with Cummy on his mature genius. From her he learned the drama and rhythm of Scots vernacular speech, gained an encyclopaedic knowledge of the Authorised Version of the Bible, and entered the frightening but imaginatively satisfying world of folklore and superstition. All of these were gains which, in one way or another, would enrich his finest work. On the negative side, for the rest of his life Stevenson had a morbid sense of sin that clung around him like a cold mist long after he had rationally dismissed the beliefs Cummy had instilled into him. He equated sinfulness with disease and ugliness, and like many other Scots who violently rejected the church's teachings, could never quite throw off the notion that he was being judged by the God in whom he no longer believed. Although 'her boy' paid generous homage to her in later life, to call her 'the angel of my infant life' was to lavish praise too sentimental to be credible.

*   *   *

So vivid are the descriptions of Louis's childhood illnesses, both in his own writing and that of others, that there is a temptation to think of him as always a bedridden prisoner in the third floor nursery at 17 Heriot Row. Fortunately that was not so – nor was it the case that his mother was never well enough to play with him and accompany him out of doors. One of Louis's earliest memories was of his mother merrily rushing him upstairs at 1 Inverleith Row to see his grandfather Balfour who had come to stay. Thus it seems that he did have, intermittently, a normal social life. Writing a reminiscence at the request of Rosaline Masson, who was compiling an anthology published in 1922 as *I Can Remember Robert Louis Stevenson*, Dr Walter Blaikie, former charge of Alison Cunningham at Pilrig Manse, told amusingly of a day in the 1850s when Louis came to tea and it was decided to 'play at Church'. Louis, needless to say, was the minister and, dressed in Cummy's black cloak and with clerical bands made of white paper round his neck, mounted the seat of a chair and proceeded to 'preach vigorously'. Sadly, Walter's mother was not impressed; coming up behind the preacher and horrified by the sacrilege of the white paper bands, the 'lady of the manse' tore them from his neck, gave the crestfallen minister a severe ticking off for his presumption and ruled out 'Church' as a game in the future. Other contributors recalled his mother running him along Heriot Row in the morning to warm him up, his attending tea parties at other children's houses and even hosting a couple of his own at 17 Heriot Row.

There were toys too, notably the painted soldiers which Louis, dreaming of the glory of a military career and adventures in foreign lands, loved all his life:

And sometimes, for an hour or so
I watched my leaden soldiers go,

With different uniforms and drills,
Among the bedclothes, through the hills. ...

– 'The Land of Counterpane'

And there was Skelt. Although Free Church member Cummy abhorred the theatre as much as she did card games and dancing and going out to dinner (all activities which Tom and Maggie, members of the relatively relaxed and sociable Church of Scotland, indulged in from time to time), she had no objection to Louis's occupying himself with toy theatres – an activity which presumably kept him from under her feet. Years later, in his essay 'A Penny Plain and Twopence Coloured', Stevenson evoked the pleasure of Skelt's Toy Theatre, a forerunner of the Pollock's Toy Theatres which were still popular toys well into the twentieth century. Skelt's Toy Theatre, made of thick cardboard, was accompanied by sheets of characters ready to be coloured (costing a penny) and ready-coloured (costing twice as much), which could then be cut out with scissors ready for use. The plays' titles give a flavour of their content: *Aladdin, The Red Rover, The Blind Boy, The Smuggler, Robin Hood, Three-Fingered Jack, The Terror of Jamaica.* 'Kits' containing character sheets and scripts could be bought (had one any pocket money) from a stationer in Leith Walk 'which was dark and smelt of Bibles'. The critic G. K. Chesterton, writing 70 years later, believed that these melodramatic scenes and characters, more than any other influence, informed Stevenson's mature work. This was perhaps an overstatement, but a line of imaginative connection can certainly be drawn between their two-dimensional, brightly coloured figures and Long John Silver in *Treasure Island*, Alan Breck in *Kidnapped*, and the wicked James Durie, *The Master of Ballantrae*.

* * *

'I have three powerful impressions of my childhood,' the adult Stevenson remembered. 'My sufferings when I was sick, my delights in convalescence at my grandfather's manse at Colinton near Edinburgh, and the unnatural activity of my mind after I was in bed at night.' It is pleasing to read the word 'delights', and certainly to Louis the cheerful bustle of his grandfather's house must have been far removed from the formal ambience of 17 Heriot Row. It was exciting to climb into the carriage with Cummy and be bounced over the cobbles of the New

Town to Princes Street and up Lothian Road, and then, as the city frayed out among green fields, to trot by woods and streams along country roads below the steep rise of the Pentlands. Colinton, now a district of the city, was in the nineteenth century an independent village. In 1812 its inhabitants, many of whom were employed in the paper, flour and snuff mills along the Water of Leith, numbered 1605, but in the subsequent 40 years the population had declined.

In a dell beyond the church, built in 1771, and sharing a wall with the churchyard, stood the manse. It was a square, many chimneyed (and in fact rather insalubrious) house described through the eye of love by Stevenson in an essay 'The Manse', published in *Memories and Portraits* (1887): 'I see it, by the standard of my childish nature, as a great, roomy house. In truth, it was not so large as I supposed, nor yet so convenient.' At its centre sat his grandfather, the Rev. Lewis Balfour, a stern elderly man with silver hair, who had traces of the previous century in his manner and ideas; he was one of the last generation of scholars who conversed habitually in the old Scots tongue, and only reluctantly preached in English for the benefit of the genteel among his parishioners. For all that he seems to have been fond of Louis, the boy was much in awe of him. All his life he remembered vividly the minister's study, a dark, cold room lined with books that he found unappealing, but redeemed by 'many Indian pictures, gaudily coloured but dear to young eyes', souvenirs brought home from the subcontinent by empire-building sons. Sometimes cousins on holiday from India with nicknames like 'Noona Lewis' and 'Delhi Lewis' and accompanied by Indian nurses or *ayahs*, were Louis's companions at Colinton. One cannot help wondering what Cummy made of these exotic foreign servants, or they of her.

Beyond the study the household had, since her mother's death in 1844, been run by Miss Jane Whyte Balfour, the eldest of Maggie Stevenson's sisters and the 'Auntie' of Louis's fond reminiscence. Deafened and almost blinded in a riding accident when young, Jane had given up hope of marriage to become not only her father's devoted companion but also the family maid of all work – a far from unusual fate for spinster daughters at that period. Described as 'serviceable and amiable', Jane bore her life with fortitude and found fulfilment in her love for her nephews and nieces. Louis seems to have been her favourite; she enjoyed spoiling him and bought him toy soldiers which he proudly showed his grandfather at the dinner table. But it was the garden, and the companionship of children who were of his own family, that meant most to the only child:

It was a place, at that time, like no other: the garden cut into provinces by a great hedge of beech, and overlooked by the church and the terrace of the churchyard, where the tombstones were thick, and after nightfall 'spunkies' might be seen to dance, at least by children; flower-pots lying warm in the sunshine; laurels and the great yews making elsewhere a pleasing horror of shade; the smell of water rising from all round, with an added tang of papermills; the sound of water everywhere, and the sound of mills – the wheels and the dam singing their alternate strain; the birds on every bush and from every corner of the overhanging woods pealing out their notes until the air throbbed with them; and in the midst of this, the manse.

Here Louis had a taste of what normal childhood was like, as he stalked imaginary tigers through the grass with his toy gun, played pirates and splashed in the water with his cousins, and climbed a yew tree so that, with his ear to the churchyard wall, he could imagine the spirits of the dead talking to him. The idyll ended abruptly when the Rev. Lewis Balfour died in 1860 and Aunt Jane had to vacate the manse, but the Colinton days, remembered long afterwards as a time of unending sunshine, inspired the most carefree poems in *A Child's Garden of Verses*.

Over the borders, a sin without pardon,
Breaking the branches and crawling below,
Out through the breach in the wall of the garden,
Down by the banks of the river, we go.

Here is the mill with the humming of thunder,
Here is the weir with the wonder of foam,
Here is the sluice with the race running under,
Marvellous places, though handy to home! ...

– 'Keepsake Mill' –

CHAPTER 3

The Education
of a Writer

At length, one melancholy afternoon in the early autumn, and at a
place where, it seems to me, looking back, it must be always autumn
and generally Sunday, there came suddenly upon the face of all I
saw – the long, empty road, the lines of the tall houses, the church
upon the hill, the woody hillside garden – a look of such piercing
sadness that my heart died; and seating myself on a doorstep, I
shed tears of miserable sympathy. A benevolent cat cumbered me
all the time with consolations – we two were alone in all that was
visible of the London Road: two poor waifs who had each tasted
sorrow – and she fawned upon the weeper, and gambolled for his
entertainment, watching the effect, it seemed, with motherly eyes.

– 'The Coast of Fife', 1888 –

IT IS IMPOSSIBLE to know just how popular the skinny, cosseted little Louis
really was with his sturdy cousins at Colinton manse. By the time he
wrote his own account, the passing years had spilled their usual golden
glow over the events of long ago, and the cousins who gave their reminiscences to Rosaline Masson in 1922 were further constrained by the fact
that they were speaking of the dead. One cousin did hint at his lack of
social skills; recalling a tea party at a house in Grange Road, she described
how Louis had been chosen to be 'mesmerised' in a game where he ended
up, unknown to himself, with sooty marks all over his face. Instead of
pretending to see the joke, he lost his temper and sulked until it was time
to go home. Here and there too, there are suggestions of his need to domi-
nate in the Colinton games, and of his capacity for sneaky behaviour; a
favourite trick of his was to run 'impishly' through flowerbeds and then
deliberately enlarge his small footprints so that an older child would be
blamed. The principal reason, however, for taking his account of entirely
harmonious relationships with a small pinch of salt is that he had such

great difficulty in making friends elsewhere. This may have been partly due to his strange physique and posh-boy clothes, but the principal reason was that he hardly ever went to school.

* * *

Robert Louis Stevenson did not learn to read until he was seven. Various reasons have been advanced to explain this late start: that he so much enjoyed having books read to him that he was reluctant to forego the pleasure; and that, with his mother a willing amanuensis for the tales he invented (in 1856 he dictated to her 'A History of Moses', and in 1857 'The Story of Joseph' and, prophetically, a story called 'The American Travellers'), he had no compulsion to write them down himself. It is also probable that, despite his night terrors, he enjoyed the daytime pleasure of invalidism, preferring lolling on his pillows playing with toy soldiers to the discipline of learning to read and write. It is well known that later in life Stevenson often had difficulty in finishing work he had started. *Treasure Island* and *The Master of Ballantrae* were only completed because the early chapters had already been published, and many of the stories he began were never finished at all. There were signs of this inability to sustain enthusiasm very early on; by his own admission he enjoyed colouring sheets of characters for Skelt's Toy Theatre, but couldn't be bothered to cut them out, and he rarely proceeded to a performance of the play. His parents, he said, complained – but one suspects not very loudly.

The great wonder, however, is that Louis had learned to read even by the time he was seven, for most of the teaching was done by Cummy, and not always with her pupil's co-operation: 'Cummy gives me my lessons,' he said archly in a (dictated) letter to his Aunt Jane when he was about six, 'and I've good behaviour ones and bad behaviour ones.' Indeed, to say that Louis's early education was sketchy is an understatement, for it did not exist in any systematic way; and for this his father (who later would expect him to embrace the work ethic like everyone else) was largely to blame. Tom Stevenson's own experience of education at the High School of Edinburgh had left him with a deep hatred of such institutions and a contempt for brutal schoolmasters; it was one of the many eccentricities of this quirky man that he would stop unknown schoolboys in the street, pour scorn on the books in their satchels and advise them to learn only what they thought good, or else nothing at all. That this subversive attitude influenced his view of Louis's education is without doubt, and the boy must soon have learned how easily he could play on parental sympathy.

The pathetic scene with the cat on the doorstep in London Road was how Louis remembered his first day at Canonmills School, to which he was presumably sent because of its proximity to Inverleith Terrace. He had been twitted by older boys about his odd appearance and, not for the last time, found himself isolated in the playground. Whether the incident with the cat actually took place as he recalled it, or whether it is rather an expression of more general depression and anxiety, is hard to say, but either way the result was the same. Before long he had confessed his misery to his parents and, despite the good reputation of Canonmills School, he was at once withdrawn and taken on holiday to Fife.

The next school that Louis attended, albeit sporadically, was in India Street, which runs at right angles to Heriot Row. A small private school, it was run by a master named Mr Henderson, and Louis went there two mornings a week, when considered well enough to go at all. A contemporary, James Milne, remembered Louis there and also at the Edinburgh Academy in Henderson Row, where both boys were enrolled by 1861. Writing 40 years later at the request of Rosaline Masson, Milne had two telling memories of his schoolfellow. One was of a summer outing to Peebles, where five or six boys went swimming in a pool on the river Tweed below Neidpath Castle. 'It was a sunny day with a cold wind,' he wrote, 'and we did not waste much time in getting our clothes on; but Louis would continue to run about and play the fool in a state of nudity after all the rest of us were dressed.' He also remembered an occasion in the Academy schoolyard when 'Louis was in a towering rage. Some of the other kiddies were ragging him, and the rim of his straw hat was torn down and hanging in rings round his face and shoulders.' A poignant impression emerges of a strange-looking child who felt compelled to show off in the presence of other boys, yearning for friends but not knowing how to make them. So desperate did he become that once in Howe Street, he ventured to ask a solitary lame boy if he would play with him, only to be seen off with a stream of oaths.

Perhaps if Louis had had some settled experience of school life he might have integrated and formed relationships, for a strange appearance need not, among children, be a barrier to popularity. Unfortunately this never happened; not only did his own illnesses disrupt his attendance and make him unfit for the games other boys enjoyed, but so did the priority given to the health problems of his parents. Frequently Louis was taken out of school to accompany Tom and Maggie to local health resorts (Bridge of Allan was a favourite), and at other times to tour the Lake District and pay visits to London, Salisbury and the Isle of Wight. Twice the family went further afield, crossing the English Channel and taking leisurely journeys through the continent of Europe.

The first of these jaunts took place in 1863 and lasted nearly four months. It was taken on the advice of Maggie's doctors, who thought her chest ailment would be alleviated by escape from the worst of an Edinburgh winter. Accompanied by Cummy and Louis's teenage cousin Bessie Stevenson, the family from Heriot Row went first to Paris then, after some weeks at Nice and Menton on the French Riviera, headed over the Alps to Italy. Visits were made to Genoa, Naples, Rome, Florence and Venice, before the return journey by Innsbruck in Austria and the river Rhine. The tour was described minutely by Cummy in a journal she kept for the benefit of a friend in Edinburgh, and which was published in a limited edition in 1926, by which time Robert Louis Stevenson's old nurse had become a minor cult figure. Not surprisingly, as a stiff, self-righteous, provincial Scots Calvinist abroad in wicked Roman Catholic Europe, she disapproved of everything, from foreign food (with the exception of some rather special mashed potato) to the shocking spectacle of women in Nice hanging out their washing on a Sunday. 'No Sabbath here in this land, where the man of sin reigns.'

It has been claimed that Tom Stevenson believed that travel was a valuable part of education, but there is little evidence that this extended holiday did much to broaden Louis's horizons. Unlike so many literary compatriots he was, and would remain all his life, indifferent to the beauty of Italy's architecture and countryside; and on the return journey, every time the carriage entered a new city, he would wail, 'I wish this was Auld Reekie!' There is, however, some evidence that by his thirteenth year he was becoming aware of the absurdity in Cummy's behaviour and learning to tease her. In a church in Nice she was curious to know what the priests were doing behind a curtain in a corner. Instead of explaining what he knew perfectly well, that they were hearing confessions, Louis told her that they were playing cards for money. 'Is it not very melancholy?' she wrote in her staid, humourless fashion.

Just why, on his return from this holiday, Louis was suddenly sent away to boarding school in England is unclear, but it seems likely that, when Maggie was again advised to go south in 1864, it was decided that Louis needed a settled spell of education after all. He was enrolled at

Burlington Lodge Academy, Spring Grove, at Isleworth in Surrey, chosen because three of his Balfour cousins were already pupils there. The transition from the pampered security of home was naturally traumatic; Louis was unhappy and by November, when his parents were due to leave for the south of France, he was breaking under the strain of separation. 'My dear Papa,' he wrote pathetically, 'you told me to tell you whenever I was miserable. I do not feel well and I wish to get home. Please take me with you.'

Unsurprisingly Tom caved in and came in person to fetch him, and by Christmas Louis was basking in the sun with his parents at Menton, surrounded by books and being fussed over by Cummy, who had been shipped out specially to look after him. The only good things that came out of his brief spell at boarding school were that he began to learn French and, even more importantly, to discover the writer in himself. Editor, and indeed sole contributor to *The School Boys Magazine*, he found his classmates appreciative readers, and had his first taste of the pleasure of publication. But again he failed to make friends, and by the following summer he was back in Edinburgh, finding refuge now in the books he had been so slow to read. Although Cummy's direct influence was certainly waning as the extreme Calvinism of his infancy began to be modified by adolescent doubt, he remained obsessed by the Covenanters, and books with titles such *History of the Sufferings of the Church of Scotland* and *Analecta, or Materials for a History of Remarkable Providences* were pored over in his lonely room along with novels of W. M. Thackeray, Alexandre Dumas and Sir Walter Scott.

* * *

It is a relief to know that, in the midst of so much solitude and fruitless yearning for friends, Louis had at least made one relationship that would last. It was with a cousin, although because it was on the Stevenson side of the family it was not formed in the manse at Colinton. Tom Stevenson's elder brother Alan had left the family firm in 1853 because of increasing debility, but three years passed before some serious crisis in his illness required the temporary removal of his two older children from home. Robert Alan Mowbray Stevenson, always known as 'Bob', and his sister Katharine were helpfully taken in by Tom and Maggie, and spent the entire winter of 1856 at 1 Inverleith Terrace. Louis, who had longed for siblings, was delighted. Both Bob and Katharine became his friends, but it was with Bob, three years his senior, that he formed the stronger bond. The two boys were alike in temperament as well as interests; Bob was a dreamy, imaginative ten-year-old who, like Louis, was growing up in a house darkened by illness and learning to protect himself by retreating into worlds of his own creation. In Louis he found an eager collaborator, and the two were constantly together, playing with toy soldiers, colouring in pictures, dressing up to act in plays inspired by Skelt. In a game reminiscent of the one played by the young Brontës at Haworth Parsonage 30 years earlier, Bob and Louis drew maps of imaginary kingdoms. Bob's was named 'Nosingtonia' and shaped like Ireland, while Louis was ruler of 'Encyclopaedia', which 'lay diagonally across the paper like a large tip-cat' (a wooden toy wide in the centre and tapering at both ends). Even the mundane business of eating porridge at breakfast was enlivened by this game. Bob poured sugar over his and said it was Nosingtonia covered with snow, to which Louis responded by pouring milk over his and declaring Encyclopaedia engulfed by floods.

It was a happy interlude, and though in the spring Bob and Katharine left Inverleith Terrace to travel to France with their sick father, the relationship proved an enduring one. The three children were again together in the 1860s, on family holidays in Peebles, and at the east coast resort of North Berwick. Katharine never forgot North Berwick with 'the long twilight on its "sands", the glen and the burn running down to the sea', and Louis would revisit it years later in one of his most atmospheric stories, 'The Pavilion on the Links'. Bob, Katharine and Louis, whose health had been improving as he approached his teens, learned to swim and to ride ponies: Bob's called 'Hell', Katharine's 'Heaven' and Louis's by the very un-Presbyterian name of 'Purgatory'.

At first Louis found it hard to break into the clannish group of holiday-making boys who knew each other from school in Edinburgh, but to his delight he was accepted once they discovered his talent for telling stories. This was a great boost to his confidence and in an enchanting essay, 'The Lantern Bearers', he later recalled vividly the exhilaration of September evenings by the sea, when the boys met after dark, with bulls-eye lanterns tucked into their coats, and crouched in the bilges of a fishing boat to smoke and enjoy adolescent 'dirty talk'. It was his first experience of being 'one of the gang' and he loved it. Again, however, the happy, normal summer interlude must have thrown into sharp relief the teenage pleasures he was missing in Edinburgh, and it was around this time that he began to regard 17 Heriot Row as a cage. More and more he sought refuge in the fantasy world of reading and writing, the classic retreat of intelligent children who find reality too hard to bear.

*　*　*

In 1865 Louis spent long periods with his mother and a private tutor in Torquay in the south-west of England. He did not enjoy the lessons and spent all his spare time working on a story 'The Plague Cellar', and on a draft of a play about Deacon William Brodie, the respectable Edinburgh cabinetmaker whose parallel career as a night-time burglar led him, in 1788, to execution on a scaffold of his own design. The work distracted him at a time of broken dreams; after a period of better health he was again experiencing bronchial illness. His excited ambition of finding glory as a soldier was fading, and the constant company of his invalid mother, must have been an unwelcome reminder of his flawed heredity.

So far Louis's parents had been indulgent towards his writing, and when the teenager came home all agog after meeting R. M. Ballantyne, author of the famous boys' adventure story *The Coral Island*, at his Uncle David's house, they were less perturbed than pleased for him. Maggie still thought everything Louis did was wonderful, while Tom, no doubt mindful of his own father's trampling on literary ambition, encouraged his son to the point of paying, in 1866, for the publication of one hundred copies of his study *The Pentland Rising: A Page of History*. This was a partisan, highly coloured but not unscholarly account of a 1666 rebellion against the Crown by some hundreds of Covenanters, which ended in their annihilation by Sir Thomas Dalziel and his dragoons at the Battle of Rullion Green. Tom Stevenson was no doubt gratified by the choice of a subject dear to his own heart but, not for the last time, he was so critical that the young author must have felt sadly cast down. To make matters worse, no sooner had the book been printed than Tom, ever inconsistent, bought back all the copies. But if he imagined that either his criticism or his action would dampen Louis's enthusiasm, he miscalculated.

*　*　*

In the same year, 1866, Louis was sent to school for the last time, to Mr Thompson's establishment in Frederick Street, which accommodated 20 pupils who were too delicate or 'backward' for the hurly burly of the Academy and the High School. At Mr Thompson's Louis was allowed to choose the subjects he wanted to study (he opted for French, Latin and geometry), but even though the time was fast approaching when he must matriculate for university, he showed no more enthusiasm than usual for systematic study. One contemporary enlisted by Rosaline Masson remembered that Louis developed an interest in wild flowers and collecting birds' eggs, while another remarked that Mr Thompson was less than impressed by him:

> During the time we were fellow-pupils, an hour every Friday afternoon was devoted to the writing of essays on some given subject. In after years I asked Mr Thompson if he had ever noticed in those written by Stevenson anything calling for special remark. 'No,' he replied. 'Except for an occasional striking phrase, they never showed much grasp of, nor interest in, their subject, nor a distinctive literary turn of mind.'

If this opinion was conveyed, as it surely was, to Louis's parents on his school report, it must have given Tom some handy ammunition in the battle over Louis's career that lay ahead.

CHAPTER 4

Work Experience

A Scottish child hears much of shipwreck, outlying iron skerries, pitiless breakers and great sea-lights; much of heathery mountains, wild clans and hunted Covenanters.

– 'The Foreigner at Home', 1882 –

IT IS DIFFICULT to understand how Tom Stevenson could ever have believed that his son would one day succeed him as Chief Engineer to the Northern Lighthouse Board. Not only was it obvious that Louis, with his emaciated, unnaturally long-boned body, hollow chest and appalling history of illness was not physically suited to the task, but Tom must have been well aware of the lurking threat of lung disease, as feared in Victorian times as AIDS is now, on both sides of the family. He knew that his wife had inherited her father's pulmonary weakness, while in 1862 he had himself experienced coughing and spitting blood. Most strikingly of all, there was before Tom's eyes the horrifying spectacle of his brother Alan, stunted creatively and worn down by years of stoical devotion to his father's wishes, living out his last days with body and spirit destroyed. By the time Louis was growing up, Tom's own period of adolescent rebellion was long over, but he could hardly have forgotten it. Yet when he himself became the father of a teenager, the fact that he had turned into a second Robert Stevenson was something he seems not to have noticed at all.

All the evidence suggests that Tom's early relationship with Louis was unconventional but close. At a time when dealings between middle-class parents and children were usually characterised by a distant propriety, Tom must have seemed refreshingly friendly and approachable to the small boy. Seen retrospectively, his casual attitude to education may have been imprudent, but it was hardly sinful, and if he and Maggie tended to treat Louis as if he were more grown up than he really was, that is a common tendency among parents of an intelligent only child. On the tours in Europe in 1863 and 1864, Tom took Louis with him into men's smoking-rooms, encouraged him to listen to adult conversation and discussed cultural matters with him man to man. As a twelve-year-old, Louis accompanied his father on a tour of lighthouse inspection on the Fife coast, and for many years, fascinated perhaps by tales of 'pitiless breakers and great sea-lights', seems to have colluded with Tom in his dream of a professional succession. Yet when Louis's dream began to tug him in another direction, in spite of all the evidence that the boy was spending more and more time writing, was physically unfit and had no enthusiasm whatsoever for the hard graft of a scientific education, Tom seemed wilfully not to notice. In November 1867, the month of his 17th birthday, Louis seemed to capitulate by matriculating at the University of Edinburgh to study civil engineering, but his heart was not in it. The scene was set for a souring of his relationship with his father – a long drawn-out process which would cause the utmost pain to them both.

The transition from the discipline of home to the greater freedom and personal responsibility of further education is a shock to many young people from sheltered backgrounds, but to understand fully the impact of Edinburgh University on Stevenson it is necessary to understand something of the nature of the Scottish university in the nineteenth century. Writing an essay, 'The Foreigner at Home', in 1882, Stevenson, having described the civilised world of Oxford and Cambridge where young gentlemen live in garden-encircled colleges and are disciplined by proctors, turns to the life of the Scottish student:

> At an earlier age the Scottish lad begins his greatly different experience of crowded classrooms, of a gaunt quadrangle, of a bell hourly booming over the traffic of the city to recall him from the public-house where he has been lunching, or the streets where he has been wandering fancy-free. His college life has little of restraint, and nothing of necessary gentility. He will find no quiet clique of the exclusive, studious and cultured ... all classes rub shoulders on the greasy benches. The raffish young gentleman in gloves must measure his scholarship with the plain, clownish laddie from the parish school. They separate, at the session's end, one to smoke cigars about a watering-place, the other to resume the labours of the field beside his peasant family. The first muster of a college

29

class in Scotland is a scene of curious and painful interest; so many
lads, fresh from the heather, hang around the stove in cloddish
embarrassment, ruffled by the presence of their smarter comrades,
and afraid of the sound of their own rustic voices. ... Our tasks
ended, we of the North go forth as free men into the humming
lamplit city. At five o'clock you may see the last of us hiving from
the college gates, in the glare of the shop windows, under the green
glimmer of the winter sunset. The frost tingles in our blood; no
proctor lies in wait to intercept us; till the bell sounds again, we are
masters of the world.

The most striking thing about this description is its air of *de haut en
bas*, giving the lie to the proud boast that Scotland has, or ever had, a
classless society. But it also points to a flaw in the Scottish educational
system at that time, that young men were precipitated into the unsup-
ported world of the university at an unrealistically early age: 40 years
before Louis was born, the writer and critic Thomas Carlyle had left
rural Ecclefechan to walk 72 miles to Edinburgh University on the eve of
his 14th birthday. It is unsurprising that Louis, who had gone to school
a stone's throw from home in the respectable New Town, and had never
been on holiday without his parents, found the expansion of his narrow
world exciting; nor that, with adolescent fantasies about *la vie Bohème*,
he should have behaved extravagantly. He set about cultivating an
image designed to annoy his elders and give offence to his tweed-clad
classmates; spurred on by the derision vented on his velvet jackets, floppy
ties, tight trousers, white socks and shoulder-length hair, he became ever
more fantastical. It was at this time that one of Rosaline Masson's corre-
spondents remembered seeing Louis in George Street surrounded by boys
shouting, 'Hauf a laddie, hauf a lassie, hauf a yellow yite!'

His air of superiority and fake bohemianism, however, were less the
cause of his unpopularity among his university peers than his behaviour
in classes, which he attended as infrequently as he had school. When he
did deign to turn up, he passed the time doodling in his notebooks and
outlining stories instead of taking notes, and thought nothing of disrupting a lecture by heckling the teacher and storming out haughtily whenever
he felt the proceedings unworthy of his attention. These contemptuous
and silly displays did not endear him to poor students whose future
depended on acquiring good degrees, and his arrogance was remembered long and bitterly by many of them. He did, in 'Lay Morals', an

essay first published after his death, express some contrition for his snootiness, even confessing to a brief flirtation with socialism, but none was apparent at the time. This is a pity since, despite a continuing perception of him as a 'raffish young gentleman in gloves', a good-humoured appreciation of people of all ranks and conditions was as much a hallmark of his writing as it was of Sir Walter Scott's.

In a small city like Edinburgh, rumours of Louis's posturing must have reached his parents' ears, but Tom Stevenson's perverse attitude to education was undented. He seems to have regarded the university as a sort of finishing school and, now that he had won the initial victory of getting Louis to study engineering, to take the future trajectory of his son's career for granted, not caring much whether the young student actually achieved a degree. Had he known that Louis was only biding his time while he prepared himself in secret for a completely different career, Tom would have been considerably less complacent.

While, largely through boredom and frustration, Robert Louis Stevenson was playing the fool and disrupting the studies of his fellow engineering students at the university, he had certainly not given up on educating himself for his true vocation. Years later, in his essay 'A College Magazine', he explained his method:

> I was always busy on my own private end, which was to learn to write. I kept always two books in my pocket, one to read, one to write in. As I walked, my mind was busy fitting what I saw to the appropriate words; when I sat by the roadside I would either read, or a pencil and a book would be in my hand, to note down the features of the scene. ...

The books he read would later enable him to write with authority on Robert Burns, Sir Walter Scott, Walt Whitman, Samuel Pepys, Victor Hugo, François Villon, Henry David Thoreau, and many others; and if he would come one day to see his youthful imitations of other authors as 'playing the sedulous ape', they were earnest attempts to learn from others in forging his own style. He was also acquiring a knowledge of the old Scots tongue, then in flight before the onslaught of 'proper' English, which in his novels and stories would rival Scott's. In this he was helped by his quick ear for the speech of the Pentland country folk he met after his father leased Swanston Cottage, a pleasant country house in a village on the southern outskirts of the city, as a family retreat from Heriot

Row. Louis's recollections of Robert Young the 'old Scotch gardener' and John Todd the shepherd, later published in *Memories and Portraits*, are among the most sympathetic and gentle of his shorter writings. But the pretence of preparation to be a lighthouse engineer was far from being relinquished, and the amazing thing is that Louis actually managed to acquire some sketchy knowledge of the subject he was intent on abandoning.

* * *

In two evocative essays, 'The Coast of Fife' and 'The Education of an Engineer', published consecutively in 1888 but referring to events 20 years earlier, Stevenson recalled the 'work experience' arranged for him by his father. This involved inspecting lighthouses and supervising harbour works in the fishing towns and villages of Fife, which he had seen across the Forth from the windows of 17 Heriot Row, 'dying away into the distance and the easterly haar' – Aberdour, Burntisland, Kirkcaldy, Kinghorn, Leven, Largo, Anstruther, Cellardyke. In 'The Coast of Fife' history breaks insistently through the narrative of the young apprentice 'hanging about with the east wind humming in [his] teeth', King Alexander III plunging to his death on the cliffs at Kinghorn, witches casting spells and sinking ships at Kirkcaldy, Archbishop Sharp dragged from his coach and hacked to death before his daughter's eyes on Magus Moor above St Andrews. 'The Education of an Engineer' deals with Louis's first summer vacation. Lodging in Anstruther with Bailie Brown, a carpenter, he at first took a desultory interest in the building of a new breakwater, but in the evenings:

> As soon as dinner was despatched, in a chamber scented with dry rose-leaves, [I] drew in my chair to the table and proceeded to pour forth literature, at such speed, and with such intimations of death and early mortality, as I now look back upon with wonder. ...

What makes this essay so moving, however, is not its tongue-in-cheek recollection of young ardour by an older self, but its power to convey, through small, poignant incidents, the atmosphere of rural Scotland in the middle of the nineteenth century:

> The weather was then so warm that I must keep my window open;

the night without was populous with moths. As the late darkness deepened, my literary tapers beaconed forth more brightly; thicker and thicker came the dusty night-fliers, to gyrate for one brilliant instant round the flame and fall in agonies on my paper. Flesh and blood could not endure the spectacle ... and out would go the candles, and off I would go to bed in the darkness. ...

The day job was less absorbing. Louis soon grew bored with his own clumsy drawing and frustrated in his dealings with his father's workmen, and it was probably at this time that he wrote 'The Light-keeper', with its disdainful punchline about being 'Martyr to a salary'. When, however, he wrote home in a familiar vein, complaining that 'I am utterly sick of this grey, grim, sea-beaten hole. I have a little cold in my head which makes my eyes sore ...', his father, tougher than of yore, did not rush to bring him back. Instead he sent Louis further north to the town of Wick in Caithness, where a new breakwater was also under construction, which pleased the frustrated author even less.

> You can never have dwelt in a country more unsightly than that part of Caithness, the land faintly swelling, faintly falling, not a tree, not a hedgerow. ... The wind always singing in your ears and (down the long road that led nowhere) thrumming in the telegraph wires. Only as you approached the coast was there anything to stir the heart. The plateau broke down to the North Sea in formidable cliffs, the tall out-stacks rose like pillars ringed about with surf. ... As for Wick itself, it is one of the meanest of man's towns, and situate certainly on the baldest of God's bays.

Yet even here the young man with a pencil and a notebook was taking it all in: the frothy coves, the whin-pods bursting in the sun, the gypsies around their camp fires in the sea caves, the eerie beauty of the fishing fleet silently setting sail under the rising moon. He noted the out-door Sunday service held for the migrant workers from Lewis, in the Outer Hebrides, who came to Wick for the summer herring fishing, the wild-looking preacher ensconced in 'a thing like a Punch and Judy box erected on the flat gravestones of the churchyard ... laying down the law in Gaelic about someone by the name of "Powl", whom I at last divined to be the prophet to the Gentiles'. He was amused by the English-speaking Caithness children 'profanely playing tigg' on the fringes of the crowd.

33

The most impressive thing was, however, the unfinished (and, as it turned out, unfinishable) breakwater stretching long and dark into the grey water of the bay, and there Louis had the most exciting experience of his life so far – a descent to the seabed in a diving suit. Dressed in woollen undergarments, a night cap and many layers of insulation, with weights on his feet and a helmet bolted to his shoulders, he was lowered on a winch into the freezing water and, accompanied by a professional diver, explored the weird world of tumbled stones, weed-covered staging and dreamy weightlessness, until at last, 'Out of the green, I shot at once into a glory of rosy, almost of sanguine light – the multitudinous seas incarnadined, the heaven above a vault of crimson. And then the glory faded into the hard, ugly day of a Caithness autumn, with a low sky, a grey sea and a whistling wind.'

The last experience of the vacation, which Louis remembered all his life, was a journey on the crowded (and soon to be obsolete) mail coach between Wick and Thurso. Beyond the desolate moors, in the half-dark of the sub-arctic night, the coach was beginning to descend towards the Pentland Firth when:

> Here, in the last imaginable place, there sprang up young out-
> landish voices and a chatter of some foreign speech; and I saw
> pursuing the coach ... two little dark-eyed, white-toothed Italian
> vagabonds, of twelve to fourteen years of age, one with a hurdy-
> gurdy, the other with a cage of white mice. The coach passed on,
> and their small Italian chatter passed into the distance; and I was
> left to marvel how they had wandered into that country ... and
> when (if ever) they should see again the silver wind-breaks run
> among the olives, and the stone-pine stand guard upon Etruscan
> sepulchres.

The pretence of engineering studies and a future in the family business was maintained for a further three years, with sporadic attendance at classes during the winters and more 'work experience' in the summers. In 1869 Louis accompanied his father on a trip to the Northern Isles aboard the lighthouse yacht *Pharos*, and the following year he visited Argyll where the building had begun on a new lighthouse at Dhu Heartach, on the fearful Torran reef, twelve miles off the Ross of Mull. Again his pencil and notebook were to hand, and on this occasion he was able to set down his impressions of the bleak island of Erraid, which would surface in *Kidnapped* and the wildly atmospheric short story 'The Merry Men'. Aboard the SS *Clansman* between Portree and the mainland, he was observed by a fellow traveller Edmund Gosse (1849-1928). Invited to give the address at the first annual dinner of the Robert Louis Stevenson Club on the 70th anniversary of the author's birth, 13 November 1920, Gosse remembered Stevenson as 'rather ugly', but noticed 'something very fugitive in his expression, something in the extreme mobility of his features very difficult for the artist ... to catch'. The two young men spoke little, but both remembered years afterwards an incident, affecting in its recall of the 'Highland clearances' of the previous century, which Gosse, in *Critical Kit-kats* (1913), described thus:

> In the course of the voyage we entered a loch at midnight, and, by the light of flickering torches, took on board a party of emigrants who were going to Glasgow *en route* for America. As they came on board, an eerie sound of wailing rose in the stillness of the night. ...

Many years would pass before Stevenson put this experience to fictional use in *Kidnapped*, when the young hero, David Balfour, watches an emigrant ship setting out for America and describes the keening at parting as 'a lament for the dying'. 'The Education of an Engineer' they were not, but the summer journeys of his late teenage years in the Highlands and Islands were invaluable to Louis the writer. The experiences gained then gave him his taste for wild scenery and romantic incident, enlarged his sympathy for different kinds of people, and honed his ability to pin down the fleeting moment in a few precise and luminous words.

CHAPTER 5

In Two Worlds

Collette ... was an unlicensed publican, who gave suppers after eleven at night, the Edinburgh hour of closing. If you belonged to a club, you could get a much better supper at the same hour, and not lose a jot in public esteem. But if you lacked that qualification and were an-hungered, or inclined to conviviality at unlawful hours, Collette's was your only port. You were very ill supplied. The company was not recruited from the Senate or the Church, though the Bar was very well represented on the only occasion when I flew in the face of my country's laws, and, taking my reputation in my hands, penetrated into that grim supper-house. And Collette's frequenters, thrillingly conscious of wrong-doing and 'that two-handed engine (the policeman) at the door,' were perhaps inclined to somewhat feverish excess. But the place was in no way a very bad one; and it is somewhat strange to me, at this distance of time, how it had acquired its dangerous repute.

– 'The Misadventures of John Nicholson', 1887 –

BACK IN CHILLY autumnal Edinburgh after his summer jaunting, Louis resumed his studies formal and informal. He enrolled for classes in Latin, Greek and philosophy as well as maths and engineering, but as usual his attendance was sporadic; on his own admission he attended Professor Blackie's Greek class only a dozen times in five years, so it is hardly a wonder that Greek remained a closed book to him. In Latin he found the simpler texts easy enough to crack, but for all that he had a lifelong love of Virgil, he lacked the discipline to be a good Latinist, and contented himself with a liberal sprinkling of Latin tags in the more mannered of his later essays. In the Faculty of Engineering he did, however, find one teacher he admired, although their introduction to each other came not in a classroom encounter but through the professor's wife.

Appointed to the Chair of Engineering at Edinburgh in 1868, Fleeming Jenkin (1833-85) and his wife Anne became near neighbours of the Stevensons. Invited to tea one afternoon by Maggie Stevenson, Anne Jenkin encountered Louis in the drawing-room and, bowled over by his 'brilliant conversation', rushed home to enthuse to her husband about the 'young Heine with a Scottish accent'. Naturally Louis was invited to dinner and a friendship developed which was cordial on the Jenkins' side, although on Louis's side considerably more intense. It is most likely that Louis found an idealised father-figure in Fleeming Jenkin, while his wife was the first of a number of older women whom he passionately adored. A keen amateur actress, she presided over a drama group and staged plays in her own drawing-room; at her invitation Louis joined, and although his acting ability proved so indifferent that he was only ever given minor parts, he vastly enjoyed the make-believe of the stage, the extravagant costumes and the champagne flowing after the curtain came down.

With Jenkin his relationship was complicated; the professor did not hide his disapproval of Louis's poor attendance at his classes, nor, as a brilliant all-rounder, was he intimidated by the domestic conversation of the 'young Heine'. Indeed, his sparky put-downs of Louis's more high-flown views on literature, drama and religion quite often led to Louis's banging out of the house in a temper. But he always returned, and when Fleeming Jenkin died, still only in his early fifties, it was Louis who wrote his obituary in *The Academy* and, later, his *Memoir*.

No doubt the elder Stevensons were gratified by the interest which Professor Jenkin and his wife showed in Louis, and approved the acquaintances he made at their house. Meanwhile, however, Louis was making other friends, of whose antics they would have taken a dimmer view. In 1869 he was elected (not on his own merit, as was usual, but rather due to the distinction of his family) to the Speculative Society, an exclusive university literary and debating society limited to 30 members, with the atmosphere and manners of a gentlemen's club. 'The Spec', which still exists, in Louis's time met weekly by candlelight, evening dress was compulsory, and the subjects debated ranged from capital punishment and communism to law, Christianity and the limitations of free will. Although Louis proved as poor a debater as he had an actor, his literary abilities impressed his fellow members, and in 1870 he was invited by three of them to be a co-editor of the *College Magazine*. From the beginning Louis suspected that the magazine would fail, which it did

(Louis had to get his father to extricate him from the financial consequences), but he loved the experience and made, among his co-editors, a
close friend, James Walter Ferrier. Also through 'The Spec' he made the
acquaintance of Sir Walter Simpson, son of Sir James Simpson, the
pioneer of anaesthetics, who lived with his siblings in Queen Street,
on the other side of the gardens from Heriot Row. Apart from his cousin
Bob, long absent at an English boarding school and Cambridge University, Ferrier and Simpson, along with Charles Baxter, a law student,
became Louis's closest friends. The boy who had hated school and failed
to make friends had found popularity at last.

* * *

In a generally admiring monograph of Stevenson, published in 1927,
G. K. Chesterton found himself deeply uneasy with certain aspects of his
subject's life after he left the shelter of 17 Heriot Row for the rowdy atmosphere of Edinburgh University. Using a short story, 'The Misadventures
of John Nicholson', as evidence, Chesterton contended that in his student
years Stevenson, exposed too suddenly to the 'sordid and squalid'
underbelly of Edinburgh society, fell in with bad company and came off
the rails morally – a view shared by other admirers who found painful
the contrast between the sweet little innocent with his 'angel nurse' and
the lanky student with his scruffy clothes, unkempt hair and swaggering,
ungodly companions. In a more permissive age, there is little to shock
the reader in John's crazy exploits which begin when, chronically short
of cash, he steals money from his father and immediately loses it. The
story follows him from Collette's 'supper-house', a brothel below
Calton Hill, via a court appearance and flight to San Francisco (where
he stumbles into yet another financial quagmire), to a villa in genteel
Murrayfield where he becomes involved in the disposal of a corpse. It is
wryly comic in tone, its only serious aspect the underlying Freudian
exploration of the universal tension and rivalry between father and son.
Without doubt 'The Misadventures of John Nicholson', which was not
published until the year of Tom Stevenson's death, reflects Louis's
exasperated striving to break free of parental control, and his father's
determination to assert it by keeping his son chronically short of money.

Yet while the disapproval of Chesterton, himself a recent Roman
Catholic convert, may seem to us disproportionate, he was right in
noting the impact on Louis of a whole new world within a short walk of

Heriot Row. From a modern perspective, what matters less is the effect on his moral innocence than the enrichment of his imagination and, in time, his fiction. For the North Bridge, high above Waverley Station, carried Louis to the university across one of the starkest social chasms in Europe, and the contrast, which would later colour some of his best writing, was overwhelming.

Until the eighteenth century the 'old town' of Edinburgh had been the only town; rich and poor lived cheek by jowl in the vertiginously high tenements or 'lands' crowding the swamp-encircled 'tail' of volcanic rock that ran from the Castle to the Palace of Holyroodhouse at the foot of what is now known as the 'Royal Mile'. Hygiene in the narrow wynds and alleys was appalling; human excretions were routinely tipped from windows, and the teetering, jerry-built tenements were so rickety that it was not unknown for one to collapse into the street. Yet in 1769 there lived in the Canongate two dukes, 16 earls, two countesses, seven law lords, 13 baronets and four commanders-in-chief, their grand apartments sandwiched between the lowlier premises of shopkeepers, publicans, tailors, needlewomen, shoemakers, scavengers and thieves.

This unusual hobnobbing was, however, about to pass into history. Between 1768 and 1800, a New Town of spacious, elegant houses and apartments, on the north side of the valley which now accommodates the railway and Princes Street Gardens, was built to a grid design created by architect James Craig. The aristocrats and the professional classes departed and, although the Old Town continued to house the law courts and the university, its tenements were left to the often desperately poor. By the time Louis Stevenson was a student, their ranks had been vastly increased by an influx of starving Irish vagrants. Paupers and criminals jostled in the filthy streets and, when the wind was from the north, it was said that the foul stink of the city reached Dalkeith nine miles away. Cholera and typhoid were rife, with alcoholism, criminality and degradation the condition of life in the closes, lodging houses, brothels and liquor shops to be found in every other close.

It is improbable that Robert Louis Stevenson, living in the rarified atmosphere of Heriot Row, escorted everywhere by Cummy and taking his holidays abroad, had more than glimpsed the Old Town from the window of the carriage taking him to Colinton, before he enrolled at Edinburgh University in 1867. It did not take him long to enlarge his experience. Accompanied usually by Charles Baxter, known as Louis's *fidus Achates* (the faithful friend of the hero in Virgil's *Aeneid*) and often by Simpson and Ferrier, he rollicked around brothels and disreputable pubs, arguing loudly, getting drunk, looking for sex. Although Louis acquired a reputation for kindliness and concern for prostitutes, he certainly sought their company and, to the dismay of his earlier biographers, there was a persistent rumour that he had had an affair with one of them, somewhat nebulously referred to as 'Claire'. This has not been proved conclusively, nor has another claim, that he had fathered the illegitimate son of the Jenkins's servant. Even so, it was surely hypocritical of him to infer in 'The Misadventures of John Nicholson' that had he had been given a more generous allowance he might have 'got a much better supper' and not lost 'a jot in public esteem'.

More important to his development as a writer than his convivial evenings, however, were the times when he prowled the mean streets of the Old Town alone. In *Edinburgh: Picturesque Notes*, published in 1878, Louis recalled the Gothic spires, the once-proud mansions given over to the poor and the rats, the children playing in the courtyards, the vertiginously high tenements or 'lands' with their fluttering strings of washing against the tall sky. His favourite time was twilight, when the lamps were lit and the busy modern city seemed to recede; that was when he felt close to the ghosts of citizens long gone, and sensed the beating heart of the present:

> One night I went along the Cowgate after everyone was abed but the policeman, and stopped by hazard before a tall *land*. The moon touched upon its chimneys and shone blankly on the upper windows; there was no light anywhere in the great bulk of the building; but as I stood there it seemed to me that I could hear quite a body of quiet sounds from the interior; doubtless there were many clocks ticking, and people snoring on their backs. And thus, as I fancied, the dense life within made itself audible in my ears, family after family contributing to the general hum, and the whole pile beating in tune like a great disordered heart. Perhaps it was little more than a fancy altogether, but it was strangely impressive at the time, and gave me an imaginative measure of the disproportion between the quantity of living flesh and the trifling walls that separated and contained it.

It is highly unlikely Louis's parents knew anything of his nocturnal adventures, since they frequently entertained his friends at 17 Heriot

Row. No doubt they were pleased by his election to the Speculative Society, and to know that Louis was associating with the sons of gentlemen. They would have been less delighted had they known that the sceptical nature of the debates, and the subversive conversation of the young gentlemen in Rutherford's Bar in Drummond Street afterwards, were feeding his youthful contempt for middle-class respectability and, worse, leading him to question the religious beliefs in which he had been so zealously brought up. It is hard not to feel sorry for Tom and Maggie Stevenson, who were genuinely devout and who had been good parents according to their own lights. On the other hand, they were hardly unique in having to cope with the posturing and rebelliousness of an intelligent adolescent poised between childhood and maturity. Two great crises lay ahead of them, in one of which they behaved much more sensibly than in the other.

*   *   *

The return of Bob Stevenson to Edinburgh from Cambridge in 1870 was an exciting event in Louis's life. The two cousins had corresponded over the years, and now fell easily back into their old childhood relationship. Bob was handsome, flamboyant and bold; he planned to study painting and was already in love with *la vie Bohème*, wearing clothes even more startling than Louis's and, since the death of his father Alan in 1865, uninhibited by lack of cash and paternal disapproval. Bob was immediately drawn into Louis's circle; the young men drank together, smoked together and played outrageous practical jokes on respectable citizens in what they would afterwards remember nostalgically as 'the years of jink and brash'. All the time, however, Louis was steeling himself for a confrontation with his father which eventually took place during an afternoon walk to Cramond on Saturday 8 April 1871. There Tom took the opportunity to grill Louis on his future plans and Louis, finally cornered, blurted out his desire to give up his studies in engineering and to make writing his career.

While the first part of this news must have been a painful blow to Tom Stevenson, perhaps deep down he was not surprised. Although ten days earlier Louis had given a short paper to the Royal Scottish Society of Arts on 'A New Form of Intermittent Light' which had been reasonably well received (and for which, through the influence of Fleeming Jenkin, he would later receive the Society's silver medal), Tom had been less impressed. Perhaps even before the walk to Cramond he had begun to accept that his dream of a Stevenson succession was over. What he was not prepared to tolerate was the notion of his only son writing for a living. Apart from his inherited belief that literature should be no more than a distraction in a gentleman's life, his Edinburgh notion of propriety insisted that a man of dignity must have a stable profession, with a steady income. Wisely, he did not insist that Louis give up his literary ambitions, only that he should change courses and study law. A rift between the two was avoided, but the only real outcome was that Louis transferred his casual and disruptive behaviour to another university faculty. Two more years were to pass before a real catastrophe in his relationship with his parents occurred.

During the late autumn of 1872 Louis, always susceptible to viruses and infection, endured his first really serious illness as an adult. Confined to bed in Heriot Row, he feared that he was about to die. His parents, programmed to fret constantly about his health, were equally alarmed. As soon as he was back on his feet, his mother dragged him off to recuperate in Great Malvern, a purgatorial experience where his only relief from tedium was to play billiards with one of the hotel waiters. Returning to Edinburgh with 'a new-found honesty', which he attributed to his recent brush with death, he celebrated by spending the last day of January 1873 drinking with Charles Baxter, returning late to find his father waiting up for him. Louis entered the drawing-room with a sense of impending doom.

Behaving in a way eerily reminiscent of Robert Stevenson more than 30 years before, Tom had taken advantage of his son's absence in Malvern to do some snooping among his belongings. In a sheaf of papers, he had found a sheet on which was scrawled the 'rules' of the L.J.R., an absurd secret society which Louis and his irreverent friends had formed. The letters stood for 'Liberty, Justice, Reverence', and to Tom's horror the first words he read were '... to ignore everything our parents have taught us'. Perhaps it was Louis's new-found honesty which made him respond frankly that winter night to his father's questions, admitting that he no longer believed in either the Presbyterian church or the Christian faith, or perhaps wine had loosened his tongue. Whichever it was he immediately regretted it, for Tom and Maggie, when the news was broken to her, took the defection as a deep personal affront.

To a modern mind the brouhaha that followed was almost insanely out of proportion. It was not only that Tom and Maggie took Louis's defection as an affront to their parenting; the deeper horror lay in their genuine, fervent belief that the souls of apostates were doomed to eternal damnation. To accept their son's loss of faith as a rational thought process, or to consider that it might have been a reaction to Cummy's extremist ranting, in which they had connived, when they were convinced that he had just bought himself a one-way ticket to Hell, was quite beyond them. It is astonishing to recall that the established Church of Scotland, to which they belonged, was then regarded as being at the moderate end of the Presbyterian doctrinal spectrum.

'You have rendered my whole life a failure,' thundered Tom, while Maggie veered between silent weeping and bouts of outright hysterics. 'If I had foreseen,' wrote poor Louis, wise after the event, to Charles Baxter, 'the real Hell of everything since, I think I should have lied as I have done so often before.'

Although the atmosphere of 17 Heriot Row was, in the coming weeks, as hushed as in a house of mourning, there is something as comical as well as pathetic in the way Tom and Maggie attempted to reconvert their lost lamb. Tom spent hours raking through Bishop Butler's *Analogy of Religion* for learned arguments to trounce Louis, while Maggie, less intellectually inclined, tearfully begged her son to join a young men's instruction class held by the minister at nearby St Stephen's church.

Louis was stricken and wrote bitterly: 'What a pleasant thing it is to have just ruined the happiness of (probably) the only two people who care a damn about you in the world', but he knew there was no going back. He endured life in 'our ruined, miserable house' for another six months until, worn out with constant harangues about religion, and experiencing 'an utter polar loneliness of spirit', in the summer he became really ill again. His parents decided that he (and probably they) needed a break from one another, so it was arranged that Louis would travel south on his own to spend some weeks in the quiet Rectory at Cockfield, near Bury St Edmunds in Suffolk. No doubt the elder Stevensons reckoned that the household of the Rev. Churchill Babington, whose wife Maud was Maggie's niece, would be a secure and tranquil place where Louis might recover his health and even his sanity. Louis, who had enjoyed previous stays with the Babingtons, was naturally eager to be off. None of them could have guessed that when he loped up the leafy drive of Cockfield Rectory on 26 July 1873, wearing his velvet coat with a straw hat and with a knapsack on his back, he was heading for one of the most significant encounters of his life.

CHAPTER 6

North and South

I must be very strong to have all this vexation and still to be well. I was weighed the other day, and the gross weight of my large person was eight stone six! Does it not seem surprising that I can keep the lamp alight, through all this gusty weather, in so frail a lantern? And yet it burns cheerily.

– Letter to Mrs Fanny Sitwell, 16 September 1873 –

LOUIS'S ARRIVAL AT Cockfield Rectory was observed from the drawing-room window by his cousin Maud Babington's best friend, who was to be his fellow guest during the next few weeks. Her name was Mrs Frances Sitwell, known to her inner circle as Fanny, and she had every attribute likely to appeal to an eager young romantic. She was separating from her clergyman husband who had allegedly been cruel to her; she was in mourning for a twelve-year-old son who had died only three months previously; she was mildly tubercular and very beautiful – indeed it was said of her that she had more men in love with her than any other living woman, and that, without meaning to, she left broken hearts wherever she went. Like his former idol Mrs Anne Jenkin, she was twelve years older than Louis, and she had infinitely more worldly experience. Born in Ireland, by the age of 17 she had also lived in Germany and Australia, and after her marriage at 20 to the Rev. Albert Sitwell had accompanied him to a chaplaincy in Calcutta.

It has been noted that Fanny Sitwell appeared in Louis's life at exactly the moment when he was he was having problems with his mother at home, but for all that he would sometimes address her as 'Madonna' ('Claire' and 'Consuelo' were other romantic favourites) he certainly did not see her primarily as a mother substitute. Although unusually shy and tongue-tied when Maud introduced them, by the time he returned from a tour of inspection of the moat with Mrs Sitwell's surviving son Bertie, he had got his second wind. By the end of the first evening Louis was smitten; an 'instantaneous understanding' had formed, and he was pouring out his heart to his new friend. Fanny Sitwell, though accustomed to the adoration of young men, knew at once that this one was special and, not long after Louis's arrival at Cockfield, was writing excitedly to her closest male friend, begging him to come as soon as he could to meet the 'young genius' who had captivated the whole household. The words 'the whole household' were no doubt carefully chosen, since her closest male friend was rather more to her than that.

Sidney Colvin, a prominent art critic who had recently, at the age of only 28, been appointed Slade Professor of Fine Art at Cambridge, had been in love with Fanny Sitwell since the late 1860s, although incredibly he would not marry and set up house with her until 1903. When he came down to Cockfield to meet Louis, he already had the appearance of a middle-aged man; tall and thin with prematurely wrinkled skin and a diffident, formal manner, he seemed more than six years older than the 'young genius' whose excitement at meeting someone who actually wrote for the *Fortnightly Review* and the *Pall Mall Gazette* was almost childish. Fortunately Colvin was not a condescending man; he immediately recognised the qualities about which Fanny Sitwell had enthused, and the seeds were sown of a friendship which was of the greatest importance to Louis both professionally and personally. At this first meeting Colvin was sufficiently impressed to discuss with his new friend possible books and essays that might be of interest to the publisher Alexander Macmillan.

After Colvin had returned to Cambridge, Louis remained at Cockfield for a further three weeks in the company of Fanny Sitwell, becoming daily more besotted. 'I am too happy,' he wrote, perhaps unwisely, to his mother in Edinburgh, 'to be much of a correspondent.' There were outings, he told her, to Melford and Lavenham, where he marvelled at the placidity and beauty of English towns. In the Rectory garden he horsed about with young Bertie Sitwell in the warm summer afternoons, and in the long, sultry twilights talked of life and literature with his new 'Muse'.

It was delightful, but all too soon the idyllic days of August came to an end; in early September Louis had no choice but to leave Cockfield Rectory and return to 17 Heriot Row. Separation did not cool his ardour nor stop his flow of words; letters to his beloved flooded daily from his pen, assuring Mrs Sitwell that sweet traces of her passage had been left everywhere in the house of his mind, that her sympathy was the wind in his sails, and that he was more inspired by her than a Christian by his deity. There were pages and pages, all embarrassingly lush and high-falutin.

It is impossible to know what Fanny Sitwell really felt towards Louis at this time, especially since her letters to him were later, at her request, destroyed. It is clear, from her brief contribution to *I Can Remember Robert Louis Stevenson*, headed 'Lady Colvin' and written when she was over 80, that at Cockfield Rectory she was enchanted by him. Lonely and vulnerable herself, she may well have responded with a warmth of affection which retrospectively she realised was unwise. Certainly her position, *vis-à-vis* both her husband and Colvin, required discretion, and the last thing she could have wanted was to become the subject of gossip in her own social circle. Yet in the early days at least, she did nothing to discourage Louis's ardour, and one can only suppose that she was pleased and flattered by it.

* * *

At 17 Heriot Row, meanwhile, the drama continued to unfold. Louis's return had been less dreadful than he had feared; his parents were surprisingly cordial and seemed really pleased to have him back. Briefly he even dared to hope that they had decided to let sleeping dogs lie. Events, however, had moved on in his absence, and this warm reception was only the lull before another storm.

While Louis was enjoying himself in Suffolk, his 30-year-old cousin Lewis Balfour, one of Maggie's many nephews, was lying on his death-bed in Edinburgh. Tom Stevenson, intent on his Christian duty, went to visit the dying man, who was still able to speak. Lewis Balfour, who apparently had a long-standing animosity against Bob Stevenson, used this last opportunity to malign Bob to his uncle, calling him 'a filthy atheist' who had been responsible for turning Louis away from Christianity and against his parents. This sad and spiteful accusation was exactly what Tom and Maggie wanted to hear, and they swallowed it whole. It was wonderful to be able to transfer at least part of the blame for Louis's apostasy to someone else, and herein lay the reason for their mysterious civility on Louis's return.

Only a few days after this happy homecoming, however, Bob arrived in Louis's room in a state of sobbing agitation. He had been collared by his uncle Tom and violently accused of destroying Louis's faith; Bob's denial that his cousin's apostasy had anything to do with him was met with angry incredulity and the interview quickly deteriorated into a slanging match which left Bob shaken and weak at the knees. During the rest of September, alongside his romantic effusions, Louis gave Fanny Sitwell a blow-by-blow account of the maelstrom of paternal accusation and maternal lamentation which followed his indignant defence of Bob, the threats and the peevishness and the sheer exhaustion of living with a man who simply could not leave well alone.

* * *

By October 1873 his father's intermittent sulks and histrionics were seriously getting on Louis's nerves, and probably also on his mother's, although her default position was always to side with Tom. Louis lost weight and, sinking ever deeper into guilt-ridden melancholy, felt that everything and everyone were against him. Despite Colvin's encouragement, the first work he submitted to the *Saturday Review*, a travel essay titled 'Roads' and inspired by his tramping the Suffolk lanes, had been rejected, and Bob was about to leave Edinburgh to continue his art studies in Antwerp. Appalled by his cousin's emaciated appearance, Bob begged him to leave home for good, but for Louis such a drastic solution was out of the question. Apart from the fact that he was still totally dependent financially on his father, he was an only son who intuitively understood, despite all the wretchedness and emotional blackmail of the last ten months, that at a very deep level his parents also depended on him.

In a partial and passionately argued biography of Stevenson, published in 1993 to coincide with the centenary of the author's death, Frank McLynn stated his view that Stevenson's relationship with his father was a classic case of Oedipus complex. He argued that Louis was fixated on the mother figure, variously represented by his birth mother, his 'second mother' Alison Cunningham and the older women to whom he was at different times attached, and that subconsciously he hated his father and wanted to kill him. It is a nifty theory, and a particular reading of Louis's letters can be made to support it. A reading of his fiction also yields pieces that appear to back it up. 'The Misadventures of John Nicholson' is one, and another is 'The House of Eld', a posthumously published 'fable' which gives a fairy-tale gloss to a horrible little story of bondage and parricide. Yet however compelling the Freudian interpretation, it remains true that on the conscious level Louis seems to have felt for his parents the universal mix of teeth-grinding impatience, frustration, amusement, pity and love. Besides, as any Scot knows, the Presbyterian conscience can long outlast the religious belief that inspired it. Louis was incapable of breaking with his parents completely, but it was becoming ever more obvious that right now he would have to get away from them. The question, as the autumn winds of 1873 began to blow dead leaves along the gutters of Heriot Row, was how this was to be arranged.

*   *   *

For the first time in many months, the tide of events turned in Louis's favour. On a train journey, he told Fanny Sitwell, he and his father had met the Lord Advocate, the principal law officer of Scotland, who had suggested that Louis might apply for admission to the English Bar. Given the pride of Scots in their distinctive legal system, it may be assumed that the Lord Advocate was suggesting an additional qualification rather than a shift from one jurisdiction to another, but it was a straw which Louis grasped with gratitude. Summoned to assist his friend, Colvin willingly arranged the necessary forms of admission to the English Inns of Court, but as the date of the preliminary examination drew closer, Louis, worn to a shred by domestic strife and well aware that he was ill-prepared, feared that this precious avenue of escape would be closed to him for ever. On 24 October he decided to act. Telling his parents truthfully that he needed a change of air, and untruthfully that he was going to Carlisle, he travelled to London and took a cab to Fanny Sitwell's house in Chepstow Place. He appeared before her horrified eyes in a state of collapse.

That there was collusion in the events that followed is certain. The doctor whom Colvin and Fanny Sitwell insisted should examine Louis was Dr (later to be Sir) Andrew Clark, a specialist in lung diseases. From Louis's symptoms – sore throat, fever, coughing, rheumatism and extreme emaciation – the doctor opined that there was no tuberculosis present, but that the lungs were 'delicate and just in the state where disease might very easily set in'. He also stated what was obvious to everyone, that Louis's nerves were 'quite broken down'. Louis, he said, must on no account suffer the stress of law exams, but must spend the coming winter resting in the warmer climate of the south of France. When this advice, which was music to Louis's ears, was relayed up to

Edinburgh, Tom and Maggie swallowed their fury at their son's deceit and came speeding to London, where they insisted on speaking to Dr Clark themselves. Attempting to regain the initiative in the face of the doctor's inflexible opinion, Maggie suggested that there was no need to go all the way to the Mediterranean; instead she would take Louis to Torquay. This is where it becomes clear that Colvin and Fanny had already spoken privately to Dr Clark, urging him to separate their protégé from his parents, and that the doctor had taken their views on board. It was essential that Louis should go to the south of France, he said, and when poor Maggie replied that in that case she would go too, he brusquely refused permission. Bowing to such forceful professional opinion, the elder Stevensons reluctantly agreed that Louis should travel south alone, provided that it was only for six weeks. 'Methinks I shall manage to disappoint them,' crowed Louis to Colvin.

For the next ten days the invalid basked in Fanny Sitwell's solicitous attention. Introduced to his parents, she unsurprisingly charmed Tom and left Maggie cold. Mother and son parted on a sour note; on the last Sunday before his departure, Louis gave offence by deciding to go to church with Mrs Sitwell rather than with his parents. Considering the tempests that had raged through 17 Heriot Row in the past year, it says much about middle-class Edinburgh's determination to keep up appearances that the 'careless infidel' still went to church at all. On 5 November Tom and Maggie returned discomfited to Edinburgh, while Louis, unable to conceal his glee, departed alone in the opposite direction.

CHAPTER 7

The Pains of Love

It is only after he is fairly arrived and settled down in his chosen corner that the invalid begins to understand the change that has befallen him. Everything about him is as he had remembered, or as he had anticipated. Here, at his feet, under his eyes, are the olive gardens and the blue sea. Nothing can change the eternal magnificence of form of the naked Alps behind Mentone; nothing, not even the crude curves of the railway, can utterly deform the suavity of contour of one bay after another along the whole reach of the Riviera. And of all this, he has only a cold head knowledge that is divorced from enjoyment. He recognises with his intelligence that this thing and that thing is beautiful, while in his heart of hearts he has to confess that it is not beautiful for him.

– 'Ordered South', 1874 –

LOUIS TOOK TWO days to reach Menton, travelling by Paris, Avignon and Orange. The resort, which the British in his day called 'Mentone', is better known now for its Lemon Festival and its connection with the French artist Jean Cocteau than for any association with Robert Louis Stevenson, although he is not entirely forgotten; in *Partage de Memoire: Ecrivains, artistes, créateurs à Menton* (2001) by Louis Nicolas Amoretti, a page is devoted to him. When Louis had stayed there with his parents and Cummy, at the Hôtel de Londres in 1862 and at the Hôtel de Russie in 1863, Menton had been little more than a small, quaint, quiet mediaeval town on the extreme fringe of the French Riviera between Monte Carlo and San Remo, but even in the following decade it had grown in popularity and size. 'A string of omnibuses (perhaps thirty) go up and down under the plane trees of the Turin Road on the occasion of each train,' Louis told his mother, adding that 'the promenade has crossed both streams, and bids fair to reach the Cap St Martin.' The

Hôtel de Londres, where he had thought to stay, was no longer a hotel, but he was able to assure Maggie that he had found a pleasant room in the Hôtel du Pavillon, with two windows and a superb view of Menton and the hills.

But although at Orange Louis had found 'such a great flood of sunshine [pouring] in upon me that I confess to having danced and expressed my satisfaction aloud,' his mood of happy relief cooled rapidly. He found himself listless and irritable, quarreling with strangers and finding it impossible to establish a routine. As he described it in his essay 'Ordered South', which chillingly lays before the reader his state of mind at this time, he seemed 'to touch things with muffled hands, and to see them through a veil'. Separated from home and friends and in the dispiriting company of other invalids, he took opium (certainly not for the first time, since its derivative, laudanum, was the only treatment available for the illnesses he had suffered since birth), but in his miserable condition it had a more potent effect. 'Wonderful tremors filled me,' he wrote, 'my head swam in the most delirious but enjoyable manner; and the bed oscillated with me like a boat in a very gentle ripple.' Unable to work he fretted constantly about his unsatisfactory relationship with Fanny Sitwell, his guilt over his quarrel with his father, and what is nowadays called 'writer's block'.

It seems to have been anxiety about money that darkened his spirits most. His father was giving him a generous allowance to live in Menton – in contrast to the parsimonious pocket money he doled out at home – but now Louis felt embarrassed about living at his father's expense (not something that seemed to trouble him unduly in happier times). He made trifling, unnecessary economies, and apologised for spending £5.15s. on a winter cloak. The root cause of his misery, however, was that two years had passed since he had decided to adopt writing as a profession, and although the essay 'Roads', previously rejected by the *Saturday Review*, had been accepted and was published in the December issue of the *Portfolio*, a financially viable career seemed as far off as ever. 'If Colvin does not think that I shall be able to support myself soon by literature,' he wrote dismally to Mrs Sitwell, 'I shall give it up and go (horrible as the thought is to me) into an office of some sort. You do not know how much this money question begins to take more and more importance in my eyes every day.' At 23 he felt like an old man: 'If you knew how old I felt! I am sure this is what age brings with it – this carelessness, this disenchantment, this continual bodily weariness. I am a man of seventy: O Medea, kill me, or make me young again!' He had all the symptoms of acute depression, rather than any disease of the lungs.

In December, Sidney Colvin came out from London to spend a fortnight with Louis, finding him 'without tangible disease but very weak and ailing'. Nonetheless the visit was good for Louis; Colvin was positive about his prospects and the two young men visited Monaco and Monte Carlo together. Colvin, who had better social contacts than his friend, took him to dine with the radical parliamentarian Sir Charles Dilke, and introduced him to a fellow Scotsman, the scholarly folklorist and poet Andrew Lang (1844-1912). Although their schooldays at the Edinburgh Academy had just overlapped, Stevenson and Lang had never met. There was no immediate rapport. Louis dismissed Lang to his father as 'good-looking, delicate, Oxfordish'; he was irked that Lang, who was brought up in Selkirk, had acquired a falsely refined accent when he went to Balliol, and later described him slightingly as 'a la-dy, da-dy, Oxford kind of Scot'. Lang was even less complimentary. He recorded that Louis was 'more like a lass than a lad', winced at his uncompromisingly Scots accent and, displeased by his long hair and flamboyant cloak, condemned him as a 'damned aesthete'. Happily, despite this unpromising start, prejudice was tempered and friendship established, though Lang never overcame his horror of Louis's clothes. 'No, no, go away, Louis. Go away!' he squealed comically on a later occasion, meeting Louis in London garbed in black shirt, red tie, brigand cloak and velvet smoking cap. 'My character will stand a great deal, but it won't stand being seen talking to a "thing" like you in Bond Street!'

Before he left for Cambridge at the turn of the year, Colvin moved his friend from the Hôtel Pavillon to the Hôtel Mirabeau, from where Louis wrote home on 4 January 1874 in a much more cheerful frame of mind.

> My dear Mother, – we have here fallen on the very pink of hotels. I do not say that it is more pleasantly conducted than the Pavillon, for that were impossible; but the rooms are so cheery and bright and new, and the food! I never, I think, so fully appreciated the phrase 'the fat of the land' as I have done since I have been here installed. There was a dish of eggs at *déjêuner* the other day, over the memory of which I lick my lips in the silent watches.

It was not only the fresh paint and the eggs, however, that had caused Louis to perk up. Living in a villa nearby were two 'brilliantly accomplished' Russian sisters, the Princess Zassetsky and Madame Garschine, who dined every day at the hotel. The Princess had in tow a small daughter, Nelitchka, while Madame Garschine was accompanied by an eight-year-old girl whom Louis at first thought was her daughter, although it later transpired that she too belonged to the Princess Zassetsky. It did not take long for the flirtatious, French-speaking sisters to start confiding in the young Scot. Louis quickly found out that the Princess had a lover in Russia. Madame Garschine, ominously, had no current attachment.

It was the children with whom Louis, who always enjoyed their company, initially fell in love, and soon he was writing enthusiastically to his mother: 'The little Russian kid is only two and a half; she speaks six languages. She and her sister (aet. 8) and May Johnstone (aet. 8) are the delight of my life. Last night I saw them all dancing – O it was jolly.' There was great merriment when Nelitchka called Louis '*Mädchen*' on account of his long hair, and soon he had lost his heart to the pretty toddler who brought him flowers and popped pieces of bread into his mouth at the table. With the grown-up Russians, his relationship was more complicated.

There is no doubt that both the Russian women found Louis attractive, nor that Madame Garschine, who was well into in her thirties, tried and failed to seduce him. What is less clear is why he chose to give Fanny Sitwell, with whom he was supposedly uniquely in love, a frank and potentially hurtful account of what was going on; how the two sisters insisted on sitting close to him, reading his palm, chaffing him about his wardrobe, telling him the intimate details of their private lives. 'I had a good long chat with Mme G.,' he wrote coyly. 'I wish I could make up my mind to tell you what she said, for I should like to know if you would agree with it. ... If I am like what she says, I must be a very nice person.' If he was trying to make his correspondent jealous, he seems to have succeeded, but Fanny took revenge in a way he could not have anticipated. She tipped off Maggie Stevenson, who fired off a suspicious letter to Louis, obliging him to send an obfuscatory reply. If Fanny Sitwell expected gratitude from Maggie, however, she was disappointed; Maggie was more suspicious of her son's 'dearest friend' that she was of Madame Garschine.

* * *

The original six weeks' absence for which the elder Stevensons had bargained had extended to five months before they made it clear that in April they expected Louis to come home. It was a moment he had dreaded, fully expecting that the hostilities of the previous year would be resumed. In desperation he wrote home testing the idea that he might go to the university at Göttingen in western Germany to continue his law studies – a disingenuous suggestion since he still had no intention of ever practising law. Probably the last thing he expected was parental approval of this scheme; when he got it he was flummoxed, got cold feet and abandoned it. In April 1874 he said a regretful goodbye to his friends at the Hôtel Mirabeau and began to make his way back to Edinburgh. In Paris, however, he made an unscheduled stop.

Bob Stevenson, who had finished his art studies in Antwerp, was in Paris *en route* for Barbizon in the Forest of Fontainbleu, where a famous artists' colony had been founded in the early 1830s by ruralist painters influenced by the English artist John Constable. This 'Barbizon School' was headed by the distinguished artists Jean-François Millet, Théodore Rousseau and Jean-Baptiste Camille Corot. By the 1870s its importance had waned but its magic lingered, and Bob's enthusiasm, as so often before, infected Louis. Enchanted by the idea of artistic company and freedom from convention, he had begun to make plans to join his cousin when a cold blast from Edinburgh stopped him in his tracks. Bob was still *persona non grata* with his aunt and uncle, and the idea of Louis again consorting with the 'horrible atheist' put them both in a spin. A cable from Maggie expressed their displeasure that he had gone to Paris at all, forcing from Louis the weaselly response: 'Well, I didn't particularly approve of it myself; I only did it to be sooner able to come home.' It is impossible not to sympathise with his peevish complaint to Fanny Sitwell: 'Surely when one is twenty-four one can do what one wants without a quarrel with parents?'

As so often in Louis's life, sudden illness made planning irrelevant. While Bob departed to Barbizon without him, he took to his bed at the Hôtel St Romain with a raging headache, nervous tics and a high temperature. The doctor who attended him thought he might have the early symptoms of typhoid fever or even smallpox. Neither proved to be the case; but even as he recovered he recorded that '... I have mucous membrane raw over the best part of me and my eyes are the laughablest deformed loopholes you ever saw'. There was no alternative, he wrote to Fanny Sitwell, but 'to crawl very cautiously home', where, he added with cool knowledge of his parents, 'not very well … I shall simply be a prince'. After a brief stop in London to see Colvin and Fanny Sitwell, he took the train north, and was back in Edinburgh by 27 April.

* * *

To Louis's deep relief his long absence had given his parents time to consider how empty their lives would be, should they lose him to illness, permanent exile, or a woman of whom they could not approve. There was a new atmosphere of friendliness and conciliation into which he entered gladly, and when they came to discuss his immediate future he accepted a bribe which, given the still embryonic state of his literary career, was really impossible to refuse. If he agreed to take the examination for the Scottish Bar in July 1875, his father would reward him with a gift of £1000, the equivalent of £50,000 in today's money. Meanwhile, his allowance would be increased to £7 a month which, by the same calculation, was not ungenerous, especially since he would be living at home rent free. 'We are all as jolly as can be together,' Louis reported to Fanny Sitwell from Swanston Cottage.

When 'Ordered South' was published in the May edition of *Macmillan's Magazine*, it met with critical approval both at home and further afield. Maggie wrote in her diary that 'I like it very much but it is fearfully sad and makes me greet', while Louis's new friend Andrew Lang remembered his first reading of it as the moment when he realised that 'here was a new writer, a writer indeed'. Louis outlined fresh ideas to Colvin while working on *Fables* and two essays; 'Victor Hugo's Romances' was published by Leslie Stephen in the May edition of the prestigious *Cornhill Magazine* (previously edited by Stephen's father-in-law W. M. Thackeray), while 'John Knox and his Relations to Women' was published later in the summer in *Macmillan's Magazine*.

When Louis went south on holiday in June, he was in confident mood, pleased to be with his London friends again and delighted when, on Colvin's recommendation, he was elected a member of the recently established Savile Club. Here he had the heady experience of meeting other literary men, notably Edmund Gosse, whom he had encountered briefly in the Hebrides in 1865, Leslie Stephen, with whom he had already corresponded, and the American novelist Henry James. A hoped-for meeting with the 79-year-old Scottish sage Thomas Carlyle did not materialise, but all in all it was a very successful visit. Until, that is, it was spoiled by an unnerving spat with Fanny Sitwell.

Especially in the absence of Fanny's side of their correspondence, it is impossible to know exactly what happened. It may be that cockiness caused Louis to overplay his hand and suggest a full-blown affair. It may be that Fanny Sitwell was still smarting over his two-timing her with Madame Garschine, or perhaps, miserable in the year when she had separated finally from her husband and been forced to go out to work as a college secretary, she was simply fed up with extravagant, self-regarding protestations of love. Or perhaps she was in love with Sidney Colvin and had never taken Louis seriously at all. Whatever the reason, a sharp rebuke seems to have been administered, dashing Louis's hope of ever being the 'chosen one' in Fanny Sitwell's life, and leaving him thoroughly chastened. Just before he left for Edinburgh, he wrote a letter of apology from Colvin's house in Hampstead to the woman he adored, blaming himself for selfishness, asking her to forget the person he had been in the past and promising in future to be a help rather than a burden to her.

It was a dignified and moderate response to a severe humiliation, but after a year of passionate idolatry and erotic fantasies, the shock, embarrassment and sense of loss he felt cannot be underestimated. The correspondence was far from being over; it would continue in full flood for another year and, ever less frequently, until the end of Louis's life. His need for Fanny Sitwell was unabated, but he knew that the tone of his letters had to change. As Louis sadly boarded the northbound train, he faced a long struggle to transmute his feelings from those of a romantic young lover to those of a son for a spiritual mother, a 'Madonna' indeed. The idea of ever loving someone else was far from his mind, and the significance of the news from Barbizon eluded him. 'There are,' Bob Stevenson had written, 'some very nice Californian men and women here'.

CHAPTER 8

R. L. Stevenson, Advocate

The weather is raw and boisterous in winter, shifty and ungenial in summer, and a downright meteorological purgatory in the spring. The delicate die early, and I, as a survivor, amid bleak winds and plumping rain, have been sometimes tempted to envy them their fate. For all who love shelter and the blessings of the sun, who hate dark weather and perpetually tilting against squalls, there could scarcely be found a more unhomely and harassing place of residence. Many such aspire angrily after that Somewhere-else of the imagination. ... They lean over the great bridge which joins the New Town with the Old – that windiest spot, or high altar, in this northerly temple of the winds – and watch the trains smoking out from under them and vanishing into the tunnel to brighter skies. Happy the passengers who shake off the dust of Edinburgh, and have heard for the last time the cry of the east wind among her chimney-pots!

– Edinburgh: Picturesque Notes, 1879 *–*

THE WINTER FOLLOWING Fanny Sitwell's rejection of his advances was a difficult one for Louis. Forced back across the windy North Bridge to the university at the age of 24, and still living at home, he tried to keep to a routine of study and reading, but often he was lethargic and battled to maintain it. He wanted to write and kept sending Colvin lists of proposals, but when Colvin actually attempted to set up an arrangement with the *Portfolio* to publish a series of essays which could later appear as a book, the aspiring author refused to play ball. 'Am I mad?' he inquired petulantly. 'Have I lived thus long and you have known me thus long, to no purpose? Do you imagine I could write an essay a month, or promise an essay every three months? ... You know my own description of myself as a person with a poetic character and no poetic talent: just so my prose muse has all the ways of a poetic one, and I must take my Essays as they come to me.' Reading stuff like this, Colvin must have wondered why he bothered.

No one at 17 Heriot Row was feeling well. Although the pulmonary illness that had confined Maggie to her bed during Louis's infancy seems to have become less disabling as time passed, Louis's letters make reference to her feeling 'seedy' and 'hysterical'. Louis had eye infections, bad colds, sore throats and constant fatigue. Before Christmas, Tom Stevenson was ill with jaundice, but that was not the only thing wrong with him. Flying into rages, brooding over old grievances, threatening to disinherit Louis and abusing his wife in front of the servants, he provoked in Louis a fear that Tom, like Bob's late father, had 'some of the family ailments' – a discreet way of saying he was mentally ill. In the same letter in which he confided this anxiety to Fanny Sitwell, however, Louis really seemed little better balanced than his father: 'Indeed, if you won't think me getting insane, I think the world in a conspiracy against me; for devil a one will write to me, except yourself. Even Bob sends me scraps only fit to light a pipe with.'

Louis went to concerts, skated on Duddingston Loch and revived his old interest in amateur dramatics, but he no longer had any heart for the 'jink' of old and, as he leant his thin body into the icy, ill-tempered Edinburgh wind, his hatred of the city and longing for the warm south rose to fever-pitch. Still in shock after his rejection by Fanny Sitwell, he spent most of his evenings with Baxter and Simpson in dismal bars, drinking too much and taking opium.

Although it has never been suggested that Stevenson had a 'drug problem' in the mind-bending and ultimately self-destructive way that other nineteenth-century writers such as Samuel Taylor Coleridge, Thomas de Quincey and Charles Baudelaire had, during his lifetime he must have ingested a powerful amount of opium and its derivatives. It is very likely that medicinal laudanum contributed to the lurid nightmares of his childhood. Certainly those described in his 1888 essay 'A Chapter on Dreams', with their imagery of endless stairs, rooms swelling and shrinking, monstrous human malformations and sinister animals, are uncannily like those detailed by de Quincey in *Confessions of an English Opium-Eater* and depicted in the engravings of John Martin and Henry Fuseli. Interesting in this context is a conclusion drawn by both Alethea Hayter and Sir George Pickering, who wrote books in the last century about the effects of opium on the creative imagination; that an artist with a fundamentally well-adjusted psyche runs less risk of long-term addiction than does a volatile and unstable one. Nonetheless, if he was imbibing opium merely for the pleasurable feelings it induced, Louis was taking a greater risk than he knew.

Only one event enlivened the doldrums of early 1875. In February Leslie Stephen came to Edinburgh to give two lectures, and found time to meet both Louis and another young contributor to the *Cornhill Magazine*. This was William Ernest Henley (1849-1903), the son of a poor Gloucester bookseller. Henley had come, following the amputation of his left leg due to tuberculosis of the bone, to have his right foot treated at the city's Royal Infirmary by Joseph Lister, the pioneer of antiseptic surgery. The treatment was excruciating and meant a long stay in the hospital, but Henley was a stoic who had been using his bedridden leisure to study literature and write poetry, some of which had been published in the *Cornhill Magazine*. Although Louis's famous charm always left Stephen cold, he thought the two young writers might get on well together, and invited Louis to accompany him on a visit to Henley in the Infirmary. The following day Louis described the meeting in a letter to Mrs Sitwell:

> Yesterday, Leslie Stephen ... called on me and took me up to see a poor fellow, a bit of a poet who writes for him, and who has been eighteen months in our Infirmary. ... It was very sad to see him there, in a little room with two beds, and a couple of sick children in the other bed ... the gas flared and crackled, the fire burned in an economical way; Stephen and I sat on a couple of chairs and the poor fellow sat up in his bed, with his hair and beard all tangled, and talked as cheerfully as if he had been in a King's Palace. He has taught himself two languages since he has been lying there. I shall try to be of use to him.

A friendship bloomed immediately between the two young writers, so open, uninhibited and loudly affectionate that some modern critics have read it as homoerotic. Henley's biographer John Connell, writing in 1949, saw it as the kind of intense male friendship commonly experienced by schoolboys, but delayed by the peculiar adolescent circumstances of Stevenson and Henley until they were of an age when such a relationship was emotionally more perilous. It is worth bearing in mind, however, that Victorian same-sex friendship, before it was highjacked in the twentieth century by Freudian theory, was often unashamedly demonstrative and emotional. Neither Stevenson nor Henley was homosexual. Certainly, in the younger man's appearance there was something effeminate, as noted by the two-year-old who had called him '*Mädchen*', but there was nothing in his life to suggest that he was ever sexually attracted to other men. The same can be said of big, boisterous Henley, who was already in love with Anna Boyle, a visitor to the Infirmary, whom he would marry three years later. Yet what was between the two young men was a kind of love. Henley saw in Louis 'A spirit intense and rare,/ with trace on trace/ Of passion, impudence and energy', while Louis was bowled over by Henley's courage and relished the loud, ribald conversation and Falstaffian personality of his new friend.

As soon as Henley was allowed out of bed, Louis lugged an armchair for him all the way from Heriot Row to Infirmary Street, introduced him to Charles Baxter, and in May, after he had returned from holiday, took Henley out driving in his father's posh barouche. Henley, a seriously under-rated poet in modern times, remembered the joy of these outings in a moving sequence of poems titled 'In Hospital':

> *Carry me out*
> *Into the wind and the sunshine,*
> *Into the beautiful world.*
>
> *O, the wonder, the spell of the streets!*
> *The stature and strength of the horses,*
> *The rustle and echoes of footfalls,*
> *The flat roar and rattle of wheels!*
> *A swift tram floats huge on us …*
> *Is it a dream?*

It could never have occurred to either that such a friendship was doomed in the long run, or that the parting of the ways would be a thousand times more bitter than the casual drifting apart of schoolboys. A significant fly in the ointment from the start was inequality of social status; although he had a writerly curiosity about all kinds of lives and in that way was not a snob, Louis was not unaware of caste. It made him feel good to be 'of use' to his friends but he was not always sensitive. There was a dangerous whiff of patronage in his references to Henley as a 'poor fellow', and there were other slighting references in his correspondence to Henley as a 'poor ass' who wrote reasonable verse, had occasional good ideas but still had a lot to learn. Aside from the fact that Henley was a far better poet than Stevenson would ever be, the hauteur in these remarks is distasteful. Fortunately Henley was unaware of what Louis was saying about him, and if there were more personal expressions of condescension, at the time he seems not to have noticed. It was only much later, when happiness and comradeship had faded and memories turned sour, that the disabled poet turned in disillusion to bite the hand that had fed him.

*   *   *

Meanwhile, Louis had at last got back to France. Complaining at the beginning of March of exhaustion and giddiness, he consulted his doctor uncle George Balfour, who immediately ordered him off for a holiday. 'Victory! Victory! Victory!' he exulted to Fanny Sitwell, and the following day (addressing her carefully now as 'Cara Madre') he added that he would be in London by the end of the week. From there he crossed the Channel, met Bob and the American painter Will Low in Paris, and travelled on with them through the Forest of Fontainebleau to Barbizon where, briefly, he found paradise. 'Et ego in Arcadia vixi,' he quoted. 'I too have lived in Arcadia'.

Louis was aware, as he admitted in his essay 'Fontainebleau', that the death of Millet shortly before he arrived – 'the green shutters of his modest house were closed; his daughters were in mourning' – had brought the great days of the Barbizon colony to an end, but he rather preferred the community without an acknowledged king. Describing Siron's inn, where he stayed among a rabble of loud, uninhibited, convention-flouting young artists, whose paint and wine-stained coats, striped stockings and bizarre headgear made his own velvet coat and black shirt seem almost tame, he noted:

> At any hour of the night, when you returned from wandering in the forest, you went to the billiard-room and helped yourself to liquors, or descended to the cellar and returned laden with beer and wine. … Only at the week's end a computation was made, the gross sum was divided, and a varying share set down to every lodger's name under the rubric *estrats*. Upon the more long-suffering the larger tax was levied; and your bill lengthened in a direct proportion to

61

the easiness of your disposition. At any hour of the morning, again, you could get your coffee or cold milk, and set forth into the forest. ... There you were free to dream and wander. And at noon, and again at six o'clock, a good meal awaited you on Siron's table. The whole of your accommodation, set aside the varying item of the *estrats*, cost you five francs a day; your bill was never offered you until you asked for it; and if you were out of luck's way, you might depart for where you pleased and leave it pending.

It seems an odd way to run a business, but this vision of the Good Life enchanted Louis. His love affair with all things French intensified, and he adored the after-dinner smoking and dancing and laughing, and drunken processions among the moon-raked trees. As he dawdled back to cold, breezy Edinburgh in the middle of April, 'a pauper once more' as he told his mother ruefully, he was more desperate than ever to be free. 'I was haunted last night when I was in bed,' he wrote to Fanny Sitwell, 'by the most cold, desolate recollections of my past life here; I was glad to try to think of the forest, and warm my hands at the thought of it.' Grimly determined, he retired to Swanston Cottage with his law books to swot for the Bar exams.

*   *   *

On 14 July 1875 Robert Louis Stevenson gained the right to append the title 'Advocate' to his name. His joy knew no bounds; despite three months of cramming, resented because of its intrusion into his writing time, he was sketchily prepared and had to flannel his way through the orals with a mixture of flamboyance and cheek. On the morning when the results were to be published, he drove into town from Swanston Cottage in the family barouche, accompanied by his parents and his cousin Etta Balfour, who never forgot the occasion. On the way back, she recalled in *I Can Remember Robert Louis Stevenson*: 'Nothing would satisfy Lou but that he would sit on the top of the carriage that was thrown back open with his feet between his father and mother, where they were sitting; – and he kept waving his hat and calling out to people he passed, whether known or unknown, just like a man gone mad.'

Of course it was the prospect of £1000 idling in the bank that excited him, not any late temptation to embrace a career at the Bar.

Which is not to say that the dressing-up aspect of the Law was unappealing; wig and gown were purchased, the graduation photograph taken, and a brass plate engraved 'R. L. Stevenson, Advocate' was fixed to the door of 17 Heriot Row.

However, before Louis could go off on his longed-for summer holiday, a cloud appeared on the horizon; Tom, contrary and controlling as ever, was reluctant to hand over the £1000. Complaining that he had already paid out £2000 for Louis's Bar studies, and that he had intended the further £1000 not as a free gift but to cover the cost of Louis's establishing himself as an advocate, he promised to reconsider only when the 25-year-old was 'more mature'. Without a private consolation prize from his mother, Louis would have been as much 'a pauper' as ever; with it, he was able to escape to Paris and the delights of *chez Siron* at Barbizon. He went with his Edinburgh friend Walter Simpson on a walking holiday, and in early September joined his parents briefly in the spa town of Wiesbaden on the river Rhine.

The autumn leaves were falling when Louis eventually got back to 17 Heriot Row, raked out his wig and gown and prepared to appear at Parliament House, where by custom young advocates promenaded in the hope that solicitors would approach them with briefs. R. L. Stevenson, Advocate was only ever offered two, both of which, according to his cousin Etta, he refused 'much to his father's sorrow'. Maggie's take on her husband's 'sorrow' was as upbeat as possible:

> For a few months Louis went every day to the Parliament House
> and it was hoped that he might carry on his writing in the library
> but he soon found it was impossible; the Parliament House was too
> pleasant a place to be idle in and he told his father that he would
> fall between two stools if he went on, so the pretence was given up
> and he stayed at home and worked busily and happily at his
> literary work.

Louis's earnings from legal practice came to less than ten pounds. Whether his father ever regarded him as mature enough to have sole disposal of £1000 is unknown, but if not handed over as a lump sum, there are clues that it was invested to give him a modest income. That it proved inadequate was due less to extravagance than to generosity, for soon the struggling author was supporting others besides himself.

CHAPTER 9

Beside the Stove

You may paddle all day long; but it is when you come back at nightfall, and look at the familiar room, that you find Love or Death awaiting you beside the stove; and the most beautiful adventures are not those we go to seek.

– An Inland Voyage, 1878 –

IN OCTOBER 1874 Louis had lingered with his friends in the south longer than his mother thought acceptable, particularly since he was due to take his law examinations the following summer. In reply to a letter asking impatiently when he would be home, Louis sounded an early warning: 'You must understand (I want to say this in a letter) that I shall be a nomad, more or less, until my days be done. You don't know how much I used to long for it in the old days; how I used to go and look at the trains leaving, and wish to go with them. And now ... you must take my nomadic habits as a part of me. Just wait until I am in the swing, and you will see I shall pass more of my life with you than elsewhere; only, take me as I am, and give me a line. I *must* be a bit of a vagabond; it's your own fault after all, isn't it? You shouldn't have had a tramp for a son!'

The parting shot cannot have gone down well at 17 Heriot Row, but the rest of the letter was plain enough. Tom and Maggie were doubtless disappointed, but they could not have been entirely surprised when, only ten days after his triumphal ride to Swanston on the hood of the barouche, Louis tossed aside the 'complimentary' brief offered to all new advocates and sailed from Leith with his friend Sir Walter Simpson *en route* for France.

* * *

If one were to ask what, in 1875, Louis had achieved in the four years since he abandoned engineering for a literary career, the answer would have to be not a great deal. He had published two substantial essays apart from 'Ordered South': 'John Knox and his Relations to Women', which was published in *Macmillan's Magazine* in 1874, and 'Victor Hugo's Romances' in the *Cornhill Magazine* in August of the same year. But even when, in the later 1870s, essays on Robert Burns, François Villon and Walt Whitman appeared, along with pieces bearing such titles as 'Virginibus Puerisque', 'An Apology for Idlers', 'Forest Notes' and 'Crabbed Age and Youth', there was nothing to suggest that posterity would regard Stevenson as more than a minor figure on the fringe of nineteenth-century literature. It is much to the credit of Sidney Colvin that he never lost faith in his protégé, and to that of Leslie Stephen, who privately disliked Louis, that he made a professional distinction between man and work. The notion that Louis had any immediate prospect of earning a living from writing was, however, far-fetched; he was paid five pounds for 'Ordered South', the going rate for such work. Thus he continued to rely on his father for what he called 'coin', and Tom, whatever his feelings of frustration and disappointment, continued to finance him.

The most important thing for Louis around this time was to write 'a real book', partly because it would mark his status as an author, not least with his parents, and partly because payment would be on more lucrative terms. Since his essays on journeys had occasioned some favourable comment, it seemed sensible to continue in the same vein. In August 1876, with his farcical career at the Bar consigned to history, he set out from Antwerp with his friend Walter Simpson on a canoeing trip, intending to make notes of their experiences and work them up into a book during the coming winter. Simpson had taught Louis how to paddle a canoe during a previous holiday on the Clyde, and the plan now was to paddle two sail-rigged canoes, then known as 'Rob Roys' and resembling modern kayaks, along the Willebroek Canal to Brussels, go by train to Maubeuge, and then again by water down the rivers Sambre, Oise, Loing, Loire, Saône and Rhône to the Mediterranean. In the event this proved too ambitious, and the journey terminated at Pontoise, 17 miles north-east of Paris.

The resulting book, entitled *An Inland Voyage*, written in 1877 and published in 1878, was enthusiastically reviewed (mostly by his friends), but it made little impact on the reading public. Among those who did buy a copy, it added to Louis's reputation as a 'charming' writer, and

65

its good-humoured descriptions of eccentric innkeepers, pretty girls, dishevelled military parades, gypsy barge-dwellers, travelling showmen, pedlars and puppeteers do show the gift of observation which he would later put to better use in fiction. The more prissy Victorian critics took exception to the author's open appreciation of pretty young women; in 1957 the critic Richard Aldington, in *Portrait of a Rebel: Robert Louis Stevenson*, put his finger on the real problem of the book:

> What in fact did they do? They went by dull canals and flooded rivers much of the time in rainy weather, seeing little but the towing paths on the banks ... until they reached Compiègne they hardly saw a place worth recording; in their rain-soaked clothes carrying rubber knapsacks they were mistaken for pedlars and once rudely refused by a small hotel-keeper; and Stevenson nearly drowned himself.

This lack of incident, along with a slightly irritating sense of bourgeois young men playing at being Bohemians, are the book's worst faults; the most dramatic event, apart from Louis's ducking in the flooded Oise, was his arrest at Chatillon-sur-Loing on suspicion of being a German spy. This was a humiliation from which he was saved only by a second humiliation: Sir Walter Simpson pulling rank at the *préfecture* to rescue him.

The two canoes, the *Aretheusa* and the *Cigarette*, were abandoned in September. On the 20th Louis wrote to his mother asking for an advance of ten pounds, and a few days later travelled south to the Hôtel Chevillon, an old inn close to the river Loing at Grez, for a reunion with Bob and his other artist friends. His arrival, remembered by his future stepson Lloyd Osbourne in *An Intimate Portrait of Robert Louis Stevenson* (1924), has become part of the Stevenson myth:

> In the dusk of a summer's day, as we all sat at dinner about the long table d'hôte, some sixteen or eighteen people, of whom my mother and sister were the only women and I the only child, there was a startling sound at one of the open windows giving onto the street, and in vaulted a young man with a dusty knapsack on his back. The whole company rose in an uproar of delight, mobbing the newcomer with outstretched hands and cries of greeting. He was borne to a chair; was made to sit down in state, and still laughing and talking in the general hubbub was introduced to my mother

and sister. 'My cousin, Mr Stevenson,' said Bob, and there ensued a grave inclination of heads, while I wriggled on my chair very much overcome and shyly stole peeps at the stranger.

Such was the meeting of Louis and Fanny Vandegrift Osbourne, then aged 37. She had come to Europe the previous year, ostensibly to study painting, but chiefly to have a break from her husband after 18 years of far from harmonious married life. Travelling with her three children – Belle, aged 17, Sam (later known as Lloyd), aged seven, and Hervey, aged four – she had gone first to Antwerp and then to Paris, where she enrolled herself and her daughter Belle for painting classes at the *Atelier des Dames* in Montmartre. There she heard from the sculptor Julian Pardessus of the artists' colony at Barbizon and thought she might join it to be taught, she wrote to a friend in California, by two landscape painters, 'rich Englishmen with titles'. These turned out to be Willie Simpson, Sir Walter's younger brother, and Bob Stevenson. By the time Fanny arrived at Grez in the summer of 1876, however, a family tragedy had occurred and she was no longer the mother of three.

Fanny Vandegrift was born in Indianapolis in 1840, eldest of the six children of Esther and Jacob Vandegrift, a wood merchant. Although she was trained by her mother in the 'womanly' skills of cooking and needlework, Fanny was a tomboy who longed for unavailable education; she read voraciously and developed some skill in drawing and painting. Although not conventionally beautiful, being too small and dark for contemporary taste, she was attractive to men and, at the age of 17, made what was regarded as a splendid marriage with a handsome 21-year-old, Samuel Osbourne, the private secretary to the State Governor of Indiana. While the seven-year-old Louis was being coddled by Cummy in the nursery at 17 Heriot Row, Fanny Osbourne was feeding her first child in a bustling American city 4000 miles away.

When the Civil War broke out in 1861 Sam Osbourne joined the Yankee 46th Indiana Regiment, but left after six months. It was a sign of things to come; he could never stick at anything for long. In the years that followed, Fanny led a life of adventure and often extreme hardship, travelling with her small daughter from Indianapolis to Austin, Nevada, by way of the foetid Panama Canal, and enduring danger and back-breaking toil as the wife of an unsuccessful gold prospector in a squalid mining camp. In Virginia City, where Sam bought shares in a mine with money borrowed from his father-in-law, things were little better; the city was lawless and full of drunks and gamblers. Fanny's father had been rightly anxious when he gave her a pistol as a parting gift.

Fanny had been loyal until 1865, when her discovery that her husband was keeping a mistress caused a major row between them. Leaving Fanny alone in Virginia City Sam went off in the huff, disappearing for 18 months during which Fanny moved with Belle to San Francisco, where she worked as a seamstress. Her best friend was a man named John Lloyd, with whom she probably had an affair. It was rumoured that Sam had been killed by a grizzly bear, and Fanny may have thought of marrying John Lloyd, but when Sam finally caught up with her they were quickly reconciled.

In 1868 Fanny gave birth to a son, Samuel Lloyd Osbourne, and the family moved to a house in neighbouring Oakland, where Fanny took up painting and gardening. By 1871, when Hervey was born, the marriage was again under considerable strain; Sam, who had found work as a stenographer, was spending week nights with his mistress and only coming home at weekends. Fanny hid her humiliation by striking out independently, making new friends among the artistic community in San Francisco, particularly the painters Dora and Virgil Williams, and a young lawyer named Timothy Rearden, whom she described as her 'soulmate' but who would probably have preferred a more physical role. She enrolled herself and Belle, now 16, as students at the College of Design recently founded by Virgil Williams, but within a year, sick of Sam's philandering, she decided the time had come for a period of separation.

Although Fanny's plan to travel in Europe with her children did not meet with Sam's approval, he agreed to fund it – insufficiently and irregularly, as it turned out; harsh economy proved necessary and the children were often hungry. After a visit to her parents in Indianapolis, Fanny, Belle, Lloyd and Hervey, accompanied by a young woman grandly called 'the governess', travelled by stagecoach to New York, from where they crossed the Atlantic. They sailed into Antwerp in October 1875, unable to speak French or Flemish, only to discover that the Academy of Fine Arts, where Fanny and Belle intended to enrol as students, did not admit women. Disappointment and anxiety about money were soon accompanied by a worse horror, when Hervey fell ill and deteriorated rapidly.

The description of Hervey's illness is horrifying, as is the treatment for what Antwerp doctors described as 'scrofulous consumption', but which was certainly exacerbated by malnutrition. At one point the four-year-old's sides were painted with a substance whose fumes stung the eyes of everyone in the room. He was given ox-blood to drink and table-spoonfuls of quinine. In January 1876 an outbreak of typhoid fever in Antwerp forced a move to Paris where, in cheap lodgings in the rue de Naples, Hervey's condition continued to deteriorate. Every few hours, Fanny wrote, he bled in a new place. The smell of blood filled the house, and '… in his most violent convulsions, his bones snapping in and out of joint like the crack of a whip, and covered with blood, he lay back in [his mother's] arms …'. Belatedly summoned by Fanny, Sam Osbourne arrived in Paris just in time to witness his child's last sufferings and death. Three days later on 8 April, Hervey's tiny white coffin was buried in Père Lachaise cemetery. Four weeks after that, having paid off the 'gover-ness', Sam returned to California alone. The marriage still had some time to run, but the loss of Hervey signalled the beginning of the end.

It is hardly surprising that although Fanny made an attempt to return to her art classes, she herself became depressed and ill, suffering from giddiness, loss of memory and hallucinations. Although she lived for another 38 years, it has been claimed that Fanny was never the same woman after Hervey's death, and that all her subsequent illnesses were a consequence of the grief and guilt she felt then. Told by a doctor that both she and her surviving son were in danger of serious illness if they did not have some country air, she remembered the artists' colony at Grez. When she arrived with her children at the Hôtel Chevillon, Fanny found no artists in residence but was assured they would presently arrive.

*   *   *

It is difficult to understand, at such a distance in time, just what men found so attractive in Fanny Osbourne. The camera did not flatter her strong-featured, beetle-browed face, but neither did she do her image a favour with her untidy hair and glum, suspicious expression. A photo-graph from the mid-1870s shows her affecting a slightly mannish, would-be Bohemian artistry of dress. She also smoked openly like a man at a time when women tended to do so in private, if at all. What the camera never caught was her well-attested sexual allure, and the first of the artists arriving at Grez that autumn to experience it was Bob Stevenson.

Both Fanny and Belle, who at 17 was beginning to arouse feelings of jealousy in her mother, were entranced by the 'gentleman gipsy' from Scotland; soon Fanny was writing to Timothy Rearden in California, teasing him with praise of Bob's graceful figure, his manly strength, and skill in music and languages. For the first time since Hervey's death, Fanny mood of depression lifted and she basked comfortably in the glow of Bob's admiration, not to mention that of his friends: 'I am known among the villagers as "The beautiful American",' she boasted, 'and they crowd round to look at me. ... Only think! Some artists came from a distant town to see me. I never dared to ask what they thought. I don't mind, on the contrary, I think it's all very nice.' Soon she was out boating on the Loing with Bob and learning to swim in a long-sleeved bathing costume and, absurdly, red espadrilles.

Other artists arrived, including the Irish Frank O'Meara and the American Julian Pardessus, both of whom instantly fell in love with Belle. By the time Louis jumped through the window in late September, mother and daughter were happily ensconced at the centre of the 'artists' colony' for which Fanny had yearned. It is too romantic to talk of 'love at first sight' between Fanny and the second 'mad Scotsman' she had encountered in a matter of weeks; Fanny was still enjoying the attention of Bob. Nonetheless she found Louis amusing, despite his puny physique which compared so badly with his cousin's, and his embarrassing habit of bursting into tears, which she ignorantly ascribed to his being Scots rather than English. During his three-week stay they spent much time lolling by the stove, smoking and trying to outdo each other with tall stories of their fascinating past. So it was that Fanny came to believe that Bob had spent a fortune at the rate of £8000 a year, had taken holy orders to please his mother, and was now, despite his physical strength, 'dying of dissipation'. Of Louis she learned that his parents were cousins, both on the verge of insanity, that he himself was dying of consumption and, crucially, that he was 'heir to an immense fortune that he [would] never live to inherit'.

It is hard to avoid the suspicion that this was the deciding factor in Fanny's transfer of affection from the handsome, manly cousin to the weedy, tearful one, but Louis was too much in love to care. When he had to go home in October, she went with him as far as Paris, where they spent a week together. Much later, both Belle and Lloyd would try to portray the relationship as chaste before marriage, but it is much more likely that if Louis and Fanny had not made love at the Hôtel Chevillon, they did so now. Louis went on to Edinburgh because he had to, while Fanny took lodgings in the rue de Douay and settled down to wait for his return.

* * *

If Louis's mother had believed, in 1874, Louis's assertion that once he was in 'the swing' he would pass more of his life at home than elsewhere, she must now have realised how hollow that promise had been. Barely two months after his return home Louis had dashed off to Paris again, and between the spring of 1877 and the summer of 1878 his parents rarely saw him. In Paris he lived openly with Fanny, enjoying the permissive atmosphere of the Latin Quarter, and his brief visits home were dominated by rows with his father about Tom's continuing unwillingness to shell out the extra 'coin' needed to help Fanny and her children. Louis's letters to his former 'Madonna' became cooler and less frequent, his extravagant names for her toned down to the neutral 'Dear'. Louis remained closely in touch with Henley, who had gone back to London some months after his discharge from hospital and was working on the short-lived *London* magazine; indeed, it was Henley who wrote the most extravagantly laudatory review of *An Inland Voyage*, and in 1877 published anonymously a short story of Louis's entitled 'An Old Song'. (Intriguingly, a century was to pass before this work was identified as Stevenson's by the American scholar Roger Swearingen, who republished it in 1982.)

Naturally, the excitement and emotional turmoil of these months took their toll not only on Louis's health, but on Fanny's. In October and November 1877 Louis suffered from severe inflammation of both eyes and Fanny was limping with a sore foot; at Fanny's insistence they both crossed the Channel to consult London doctors. This was how Fanny first met Louis's friends, including Sidney Colvin and Fanny Sitwell. She could not deny that they were kind and attentive, but it was painfully clear that there was to be no meeting of minds between the dark little American who reminded Colvin forcefully of Napoleon Bonaparte and those she described as 'curious people ... the leaders of the Purists'.

Back in Paris, Louis had another spell of pulmonary illness which left him shivery and weak. No sooner had he recovered than Fanny sank into the depression which she had suffered after Hervey's death and which would plague her periodically all her life. 'Her nerves are quite gone,' Louis wrote wretchedly to Fanny Sitwell, 'one day I find her in heaven, the next in hell.' By that time their love affair was common knowledge; in a letter to Henley, written during one of his brief visits home, Louis had described himself as a 'widower' and complained of going to bed 'where there is no dear head on the pillow'.

The truth could not be withheld indefinitely from Louis's parents either, and there was sufficient consternation at 17 Heriot Row for Tom Stevenson, a well-known hater of travel, to rush to Paris in the middle of winter to find out what was going on. Somehow a total breach was again avoided; perhaps Louis went out of his way to be conciliatory, perhaps Tom proved more accepting of the situation than had seemed likely – although later events suggest that he returned home with the false impression that Louis had no thoughts of marriage. No sooner was this crisis past than another erupted; Sam Osbourne announced suddenly that unless Fanny returned home immediately he would withdraw her paltry allowance.

It is amazing that in the midst of so many troubles Louis found time and energy to write, but apart from his need to earn, work was probably his chief solace. *An Inland Voyage* was completed and, encouraged by Henley and Leslie Stephen, he published three substantial short stories: 'A Lodging for the Night', inspired by his research for an essay about the vagabond poet François Villon, 'The Sire de Malétroit's Door', and 'Will o' the Mill', the strange, atmospheric and still popular tale of an unadventurous miller who finds excuses never to travel beyond his own valley until Death arrives in a coach to fetch him.

> One of the servants awoke ... and heard the noise of horses pawing before he dropped asleep again; all down the valley that night there was a rushing as of a smooth and steady wind descending towards the plain; and when the world rose next morning, sure enough Will o' the Mill had gone at last upon his travels.

The summer of 1878 was again spent in the inn at Grez, but the merry days when Louis had found Love, not Death, waiting beside the stove were not repeated. In August, against all Louis's anguished pleadings, Fanny decided to return with her children to California. She tried to soothe Louis by pointing out that in America divorce was easier than in England, but Louis, knowing how frequently she and Sam Osbourne had been reconciled in the past, was jealous and terrified that it would happen again. He crossed the Channel to see the Osbournes off on the train from London to Southampton, but felt too choked by grief and anger to stay at the station and wave goodbye. Long afterwards, Lloyd remembered the thin figure walking away down the platform without a single backward glance.

CHAPTER 10

The Travelling Mind

Of where or how, I nothing know;
And why, I do not care;
Enough if, even so,
My travelling eyes, my travelling mind, can go
By flood and field and hill, by wood and meadow fair,
Beside the Susquehannah and along the Delaware.

– Enclosed in a letter to Sydney Colvin, 20 August 1879 –

THE IDEA OF returning either to Edinburgh or Grez was abhorrent to Louis; he wanted neither sympathy nor advice. Yearning to lick his wounds in solitude he headed south through France, and within a week of the Osbournes' departure was at Le Monastier-sur-Gazeille, a small town 15 miles from Le Puy in the Haut-Loire. Shunning his fellow guests at the inn, he tried to apply himself to work; he had stories on hand which Henley was publishing in the *London* magazine as 'Latter-Day Arabian Nights', and was finishing for the *Portfolio* the bitter-sweet essays later published in book form as *Edinburgh: Picturesque Notes*. It was a time of introspective misery for Louis whose life, in contrast to those of his friends, seemed to be going nowhere; Charles Baxter was married and about to become a father, while Henley and Gosse were both happily married. Just then, even the incomplete relationship of Colvin and Fanny Sitwell seemed enviable.

Louis was soon bored by his humdrum existence at Monastier. Overwhelmed by the need for physical activity, he decided to take a walking tour through the adjacent Cévennes, a high, bleak and sparsely populated area of the Massif Central not unlike the Highlands of Scotland. He knew of the area's history as a stronghold of the Protestant Huguenots during the reign of Louis XIV, and how the rebellion of the 'Camisards' had been ruthlessly suppressed by the superior Catholic forces of the king; the author of *The Pentland Rising* could not fail to find parallels. He also knew, after *An Inland Voyage*, that he could make a book out of such an experience, and in many ways *Travels with a Donkey in the Cévennes* has much the same mixture of description, character observation and philosophising on life and love. What makes it a far better read is that Modestine, the donkey Louis bought to carry his camping gear, is a much more entertaining companion than the Edinburgh baronet Walter Simpson. Stubborn, wayward, indifferent to praise or blame, Modestine dominates the book, and the image of her, 'not much bigger than a dog, the colour of a mouse', loaded with bedding, clothing, books, bread, tinned sausage, mutton and bottles of wine, setting her own pace while Louis loped behind her shouting '*Proot! Proot!*' is unforgettable. By the time they arrived in Saint-Jean-du-Garde twelve days later, Modestine had covered, reluctantly, over 120 miles of barren countryside, but Louis, his unhappiness unassuaged by nights of sleeping under the stars, felt no sense of achievement. Parting with Modestine for 30 francs less than he paid for her, he made his way dismally back to London and stayed with the Henleys in Shepherd's Bush before visiting Colvin in Cambridge.

Other friends and relations were in London at that time. Among them were Bob Stevenson and his sister Katharine, who was separating from her husband, Sydney de Mattos, after only four years of marriage. Through Louis, she and Bob too had become friendly with the Henleys, and when they all met at Shepherd's Bush Louis's misery must have been plain to see. The entire group had their troubles: Katharine was trying to break into journalism to support herself and her children, but finding it difficult; Bob had long since frittered away his patrimony; and Henley was always struggling to make ends meet. In one of his many quixotically generous gestures, Louis promised them all support; writing to Charles Baxter, whom he had put in charge of his financial affairs, he ordered him to raise money through the sale of 'the Debenture', which was presumably what remained of the disputed £1000.

It was at this point that Henley, remembering the draft of a play about Deacon William Brodie which Louis had written as a schoolboy and presumably shown to Henley in Edinburgh, suggested that they should collaborate in making it ready for the stage. Whether or not Louis shared Henley's belief that there was vast and easy money to be made in the theatre, he was in the mood to forget his woes in such a wheeze. In January Henley was his guest at Swanston Cottage, and their enjoyment in the work and each other's company is clear from a euphoric letter to Colvin in which Louis wrote, 'Act III is done. And the last tableau is the most passionate thing in the Drama since the Elizabethans' – a fatuous judgement endorsed by his collaborator. 'It's quite the most path breaking and epoch marking work ever produced,' gushed Henley.

Presumably they were drunk at the time. *Deacon Brodie, or The Double Life* is a disaster of a play, full of flat dialogue, unconvincing characters and a stunning ignorance of stagecraft. The 1870s and 1880s are not remembered as a high point in British theatre, but even then, like Henley and Stevenson's further play scripts – *Beau Austin*, *Admiral Guinea* and *Macaire* – *Deacon Brodie* did not deserve even the limited performance it was given. The plays would also become a bone of contention between the authors when Louis's enthusiasm for the project cooled, but that was a distant prospect when Henley hobbled onto the London train and Louis went home to get on with other work. He was now into his stride with fiction; in the next few months he added to his tally of creative work 'Providence and the Guitar' and one of his most atmospheric extended tales, 'The Pavilion on the Links', set among the dunes of the East Lothian coast where he had spent holidays as a boy.

When summer came Louis went south to stay with the Gosses, amusing their children with tales of pirates and shipwrecks that six-year-old Philip Gosse would remember all his life. Edmund Gosse called Louis 'the General Exhilarator', proving how well he concealed his depression. In fact, the sight of happy families only made his own plight more poignant. It had taken Fanny the best part of a year to tear herself away from her husband and move to Monterey, 85 miles south of San Francisco on the Pacific Coast. Even then, Sam continued to visit her. She remained irresolute and divorce did not seem to be in her mind. The resentment that Louis's friends were beginning to express on his behalf could only have added to his misery.

In the spring of 1879 Louis was ill. He blamed stress and the non-arrival of letters from California, but that was not enough to cause the alarming symptoms he disclosed to Colvin in April – weakness, languor, loss of appetite, a swollen testicle and irritation of what he called the 'spermatic cord'. Since four months later he was complaining to Henley of 'an unparalleled skin irritation' which prevented him from sleeping, modern biographers have asked what previously would have been a taboo question: did Stevenson suffer from syphilis? Considering the amount of unprotected sex he had had in his student days, this seems not unlikely; but other explanations have been offered, such as mercury poisoning from patent medication. If he did have a chronic venereal disease, however, it could only have undermined his already indifferent constitution. A visit with his parents to the Shandon Hydropathic Hotel at Gairloch improved neither his health nor his temper, and he went on to spend a bored and irritable six weeks in London, seeing friends and lounging at the Savile Club. Meanwhile news from Monterey was sporadic; when she did write, Fanny complained of illness, and the hysterical tone of her letters suggested another episode of mental distress. Whether, as legend has it, she actually sent a cable to Swanston Cottage asking for help, or whether the prospect of another spa holiday with his parents was just too much for him, at the end of July Louis cracked. Waiting until they were at Waverley Station to tell Tom and Maggie that he had been called to London on urgent business, he shooed them onto a train to Cumberland and again went south, determined to travel to California and sort matters out with Fanny once and for all.

None of Louis's London friends liked his plan, even the half-version he chose to reveal to them. Colvin hectored and Henley spluttered, while Gosse told Louis bluntly that he was mad. It was all in vain. On 7 August Colvin and Henley went grumpily to St Pancras to see him off on the train to Greenock, where he was to embark on the SS *Devonia*. On 16 August Henley revealed Louis's economy with the truth to Charles Baxter:

> He promised us he wouldn't go any further than New York, so that, whether he does any good or not, I hardly think he'll do any harm ... after all, it was his duty, and to have done it will comfort him and cheer him up a great deal. They may never meet, but I know he'll be happier for the step he's taken, and that is enough. When we see him again he will be better and stronger than ever. I hoped she would have been brave and generous enough to have given him up; – to have shown herself worthy of him by putting herself out of his way for ever. But she's not, and there's an end on't. So far as I can see, the one thing to be feared for him is that he may be induced to go on to Monterey, and there get mixed up once more in the miserable life of alarms and lies and intrigue that he led in Paris. If he don't do that, I've not much fear for him. It will end in a book, I expect, and a happier way of life. If it comes to the worst ... we shall lose the best friend man ever had; but we won't. And we may keep our pistols in our pockets.

The tensions of this letter, hope and fear, love and loathing, did not bode well for harmony in the future. Nor did the fact that by 16 August Louis was on the high seas, without even having told his parents that he was going.

*   *   *

The cheapest fare for the ten-day passage on the SS *Devonia* from the Clyde to New York was six pounds, which bought 'steerage' accommodation, overcrowded, insanitary and without a shred of privacy, in the bowels of the ship; passengers even had to provide their own bedding and utensils. For an extra two pounds a single 'second cabin' could be obtained, on the same low level but separated from steerage by thin partitions. Louis paid the extra charge grudgingly, only because he wanted to write during the voyage and the second cabin was equipped with a table and chair, as well as blankets and crockery which he did not possess. Even in this 'modified oasis' he could hear every sound from the steerage next door, the babble of tongues from every country in Europe, the wailing of children, the vomiting of the seasick, the unmistakable explosions of humans defecating into tin pails. The food served by supercilious stewards both in steerage and second cabin was disgusting; a brew so sludgy as to be indistinguishable as tea or coffee, porridge, watery soup and Irish stew, and pieces of meat suspiciously like scrapings from the plates of first-class passengers upstairs.

Louis was working on 'The Story of a Lie', a tale of a young man at loggerheads with his father; he apologised to Colvin for his bad handwriting, blaming 'the ship's misconduct'. With a lack of snobbery and a remarkable tolerance of bad smells, he went among his steerage shipmates, talking and joining in their nostalgic evening 'singalongs', noting impressions which he would record in the book which Henley rightly prophesied would be a fruit of his experience. He disembarked at New York on 18 August, having lost a stone in weight, suffering from a ten-day constipation and covered with a rash that 'stung like a whiplash'.

Having dined in a 'reasonable' French restaurant, Louis spent the night in a cheap lodging house with a fellow-emigrant named Jones. He was too itchy to sleep, and spent the next day rushing frantically in teeming rain between bank and bookshop, where he bought all six volumes of George Bancroft's *History of the United States*. At the post office he picked up letters, including one from Fanny which told him she had 'inflammation of the brain', a diagnosis so alarming that he immediately changed his plans. Instead of staying over in the city, he would leave that very night for California. The most provoking thing was having to leave the clothes he was wearing behind at his lodgings because they were too sodden to pack. In the evening, carrying a rug, his copies of Bancroft and a small valise, he joined the bedraggled, shambling queue of passengers waiting to cross the Hudson river to the railway depot in Jersey City. What happened next makes the voyage in the SS *Devonia* sound like a pleasure cruise.

> People pushed, and elbowed and ran, their families following how they could. Children fell, and were picked up, to be rewarded by a blow. One child, who had lost her parents, screamed steadily and with increasing shrillness, as though verging towards a fit; an official kept her by him, but no one else seemed so much as to remark her distress; and I am ashamed to say that I ran among the rest. ... There was no waiting-room, no refreshment-room; the cars were locked; and for at least another hour, or so it seemed, we had to camp upon the draughty, gas-lit platform. I sat on my valise, too crushed to observe my neighbours, but as they were all cold, wet and weary ... I believe they could have been no happier than myself. I bought half a dozen oranges from a boy. ... As only two of them had even a pretence of juice, I threw the other four under the cars, and beheld, as in a dream, grown people and children groping on the track after my leavings.

It was the prelude to a nightmare journey in claustrophobic railroad cars, over the transcontinental track completed only ten years previously. The passengers were herded like cattle, single men segregated from families and white people from the Chinese. The seating was uncomfortable, sleep almost impossible; each car had its own stove and there was one tin washbowl among four. The scenery was by turns breathtakingly beautiful and dryly desolate; the Susquehanna valley of which he wrote to Colvin had 'an inland sweetness to one newly from the sea; it smelt of woods, rivers and the delved earth,' while Wyoming seemed 'all ghostly deserts, sage brush and alkali ... a sad corner of the world'. By the time he got to Chicago, Louis was exhausted and malnourished; at Laramie he became seriously ill, though his sufferings caused little concern to his companions, who had troubles of their own. 'My illness is a subject of great mirth to some of my fellow travellers,' he told Henley, 'and I smile rather sickly at their jests.'

It was at this nadir in his health and fortunes that he drafted his most famous poem, the 'Requiem' which would be inscribed on his grave:

Under the wide and starry sky,
Dig the grave and let me lie.
Glad did I live and gladly die,
And I lay me down with a will.

This be the verse you grave for me:
Here he lies where he longed to be;
Home is the sailor, home from the sea
And the hunter home from the hill.

The sight of San Francisco Bay gleaming in the September sun, and the beautiful city rising into hills golden with ripe corn, put heart into the sick man, though he had no time to explore. Desperate for journey's end, he immediately took a train down the coast to its terminus at Salinas, then travelled on by stagecoach to the little Hispanic town of Monterey. After a stiff drink at a saloon to steady his nerves, he took directions to Fanny's house, a neat little adobe cottage with roses growing on a trellis along its wall. Lloyd Osbourne, then aged eleven, recalled the arrival of his lost friend: 'I remember him walking into the room and the outcry of delight that greeted him, the incoherence of laughter, the tears, the heart-swelling joy of reunion.' Louis must have thought in that rapturous moment that all his troubles were over, but he was soon to be disillusioned.

It is only fair, when critical of Fanny's lack of immediate commitment, to try to see matters at that juncture from her point of view. In Sam Osbourne she had a far from perfect husband, but he was healthy and kept a roof over her head; he was the father of her children and, had she not felt some residual affection for him, she would not have returned to California at all. Louis, on the other hand, looked to be at death's door; he was like a ghost already, with his clothes hanging in folds on his emaciated body, his feverish eyes enormous in his pale, bony face. It could hardly have escaped hard-headed Fanny that if he had really fallen out with his parents, they might disinherit him, so that, even if he lived, her dreams of a vast fortune would never be realised. At the same time, it is impossible not to pity Louis's pain and chagrin when he realised that Fanny had not even begun to petition for a divorce from Sam. He had come so far and suffered so much to be with her.

In the short term there was the problem of where Louis would live; Monterey was not Paris, and Fanny would not prejudice her reputation, and her position *vis-à-vis* Sam, by accommodating him. He found cheap lodgings in the town, hoping to visit Fanny daily, but when he heard that Sam Osbourne was due any day to visit his family, he proudly declined to stay. The sense of someone approaching the end of his tether is strong in the note he penned to Charles Baxter on 9 September: '… My news is nil. I know nothing. I go out camping, that's all I know; today I leave and shall likely be three weeks in camp. I shall send you a letter from there with more guts than this and now say goodbye to you, having had the itch and a broken heart.'

Just as the previous year he had escaped into the Cévennes with Modestine, Louis now set out into the Carmel Valley with a spring wagon and two horses. The difference was that the journey with Modestine had been prepared to the last detail; now Louis, desperate to avoid Sam Osbourne and almost mad with grief, had no idea where he was heading and took hardly any equipment at all. On the first evening out from Monterey, he left the trap and one horse at a farm, riding on with the other through the pine and cypress groves. From the railroad he had written to Colvin: 'I had no idea how easy it would be to commit suicide,' and that was what he seemed to be doing now. He had travelled a mere 18 miles from Monterey when, having neither slept nor eaten for four days: 'Two nights I lay under a tree,' he recalled, '… doing nothing but fetch water for myself and my horse, light a fire and make coffee, and all night awake hearing the goat bells ringing and the tree frogs singing when each new noise was enough to drive me mad.'

Louis owed his life to an elderly bear hunter called Anson Smith, a veteran of the 1840s Mexican war, who providentially came by, pronounced him 'real sick', and carried him to his base at a nearby angora goat ranch. Here, with the help of a native American known only as Tom, Smith dosed him with folk remedies until his fever subsided. During his convalescence, Louis paid for his keep by giving the ranchers' children reading lessons, and by the beginning of October was well enough to return to Monterey. He had experienced a close brush with death, but at least it had a positive result. Shocked by the realisation that she had almost lost the power of choice, Fanny at last made up her mind to marry him.

CHAPTER 11

Families

Our friendship was not only founded before we were born by a community of blood, but is in itself near as old as my life. It began with our early ages, and, like a history, has been continued to the present time. Although we may not be old in the world, we are old to each other, having been so long intimates. We are now widely separated, a great sea and continent intervening; but memory, like care, mounts into iron ships and rides post behind the horseman. Neither time nor space nor enmity can conquer old affection; and as I dedicate these sketches, it is not to you only, but to all in the old country, that I send the greeting of my heart.

– 'To Robert Alan Mowbray Stevenson',
dedication of The Amateur Emigrant, 1879 –

THE DESTRUCTION OF every letter Louis sent his parents between July 1879, when he gave them the slip at Waverley Station, and July 1880 speaks eloquently of the hurt and sense of betrayal his behaviour caused them. It is impossible not to sympathise; the New Town of Edinburgh was a small and gossipy conclave in which the Stevensons and their eccentric offspring were well-known. Their efforts to cover up the defection of their only son, in pursuit of a married woman only ten years younger than his mother, must have been as intolerable as they were in vain. Louis had given Colvin a note to send on to his parents once he was safely out of the country, but declined to give them a forwarding address, thus putting his father in the humiliating position of having to use Charles Baxter and Sidney Colvin as go-betweens. Tom's first pathetic idea was to try, through Baxter, to lure Louis back with the promise that £20 in Bank of England notes would be waiting in New York so that he could travel home first class; Tom rightly suspected the outward voyage had been 'on the cheap', although mercifully he did not know the half of it.

It was November before the parents, at first genuinely concerned as much for Louis's fragile health as their own social predicament, became fully aware that their son was intent on marrying Mrs Osbourne. By that time beyond rational thought, they rejected such an outcome with every Presbyterian fibre of their being, as being no better than adultery. Embarrassment turned to hysteria: 'For God's sake, use your influence,' Tom begged Colvin. 'Is it fair that we should be half murdered by his conduct?' Within a month he was muttering about being forced to leave Edinburgh and set up somewhere in England where he was unknown, prompting Henley to remark that he did not know whether father or son was closer to lunacy. 'There isn't much to choose,' he concluded sagely. When even a telegram containing the barefaced lie that Tom was at death's door and required his son's immediate return failed to move the emigrant, Tom and Maggie retired, for the moment, from the fray.

Meanwhile, on the other side of the world, Louis was being absorbed into the very different family that would quite soon be his own. Fanny's 24-year-old sister Nellie was living with her in Monterey, while she prepared to marry Alfredo Sanchez, the saloon barman who had served Louis on the day of his arrival. Louis got on well with Nellie, who would one day name her son after him. Belle Osbourne, whom he had known in Grez, proved more of a problem. Her love affair with Frank O'Meara over, Belle had transferred her affections to Joe Strong, a local artist of whom Fanny deeply disapproved; well aware of Belle's attractiveness, her mother planned a grander marriage than she was likely to enjoy with feckless, penniless and not particularly talented Joe. The matter was taken out of Fanny's hands when, with Sam Osbourne's connivance, Belle and Joe were secretly married; this betrayal brought on one of Fanny's many illnesses, and caused a breach between mother and daughter which was never entirely healed. Louis, stuck in Monterey while he waited for Fanny's divorce, could hardly avoid being drawn into the controversy on Fanny's side, which resulted in Belle taking a strong dislike to her future stepfather.

Louis had other worries too. As a source of 'coin' his father had dried up, and he was constantly having to ask Charles Baxter to advance sums from his rapidly dwindling funds; even the bare room he was renting at the downmarket French Hotel in Monterey cost more than he could afford. The only daily meal he bought was breakfast at the restaurant kept by an expatriate Frenchman, Jules 'Papa' Simoneau, to whom Louis was indebted for many acts of kindness, and whom he repaid with copies of his books for the rest of his life. The clientele at Simoneau's was rough and multilingual – fishermen, the local baker and barber and, more exotically, the captain of a whaler. Louis, with his fondness for the *outré*, enjoyed the company, noting with amusement that whether they spoke French, Spanish or Italian, everyone swore in English. They liked him too, though he never found out just how much he owed them; shocked by the Scot's starved appearance, a group of regulars secretly clubbed together to give two dollars each week to the editor of the local newspaper, so that he could employ Louis as a contributor.

Back at the French Hotel, Louis worked as usual, drafting the first part of the travel book which would become *The Amateur Emigrant*, completing 'The Story of a Lie' begun on the SS *Devonia,* and beginning a novella unpromisingly titled 'Arizona Breckonridge, or A Vendetta in the West'. When he was not writing, Louis spent hours walking on the Pacific shore, which he loved, sometimes with the devoted Lloyd at his heels, sometimes alone. Long afterwards, in one of the 'Envoys' to *A Child's Garden of Verses*, dedicated to Nellie Sanchez's son Louis, he poignantly recalled time and place:

> *Now that you have learned your lesson, lay it down and go and*
> *   play,*
> *Seeking shells and seaweed on the sands of Monterey,*
> *Watching all the mighty whalebones, lying buried by the breeze,*
> *Tiny sand-pipers, and the huge Pacific seas.*
>
> *And remember in your playing, as the sea-fog rolls to you,*
> *Long ere you could read it, how I told you what to do;*
> *And that while you thought of no one, nearly half the world away*
> *Someone thought of Louis on the beach of Monterey!*

Fanny's divorce came though on 12 December. Immediately she packed up and returned, with Nellie, Lloyd and assorted family pets, to East Oakland on San Francisco Bay. Sam Osbourne, never an ungenerous man, had agreed to support his former wife and her entourage until her remarriage, but Fanny seemed in no hurry, and when shortly afterwards Sam lost his job at the District Court, Louis found himself supporting the whole ménage. He himself moved into a room at 608 Bush Street, San Francisco, a house belonging to an Irish couple named Carson, where he replicated the frugal routine established in Monterey. He ate at

Donnadieu's restaurant, where a dinner of sorts could be obtained for 50 cents, a meal supplemented only by a roll and coffee later in the day. He took walks, enjoying the magical ambience of the 'New Pacific Capital', of which he wrote in an essay published in *The Magazine of Art* in 1883:

> The air is fresh and salt, as if you were at sea. On the one hand is Oakland, gleaming white among its gardens. On the other, to sea-ward, hill after hill is crowded and crowned with the palaces of San Francisco; its long streets lie in regular bars of darkness, east and west, across the sparkling picture; a forest of masts bristles like bulrushes about its feet; nothing remains of the days of Drake but the faithful trade-wind scattering the smoke, the fogs that will begin to muster about sundown, and the fine bulk of Tamalpais looking down on San Francisco, like Arthur's Seat on Edinburgh.

No amount of natural beauty, however, could compensate for Louis's anxiety, loneliness and sense of dislocation at this time; his income from writing in the previous year had been little over £100, Colvin was sniffy about the American bias of his essays, and he was seeing far less of Fanny than he had hoped. It is clear retrospectively that a crisis was approaching, and it seems to have been precipitated in February 1880 by the illness of the Carsons' four-year-old son, who came close to death with pneumonia. Louis, ever sympathetic to children, offered to sit up with the little boy at night and, in his debilitated state, was profoundly distressed by the suffering he witnessed. 'O, never any family for me! I am cured of that,' he wrote bleakly to Colvin.

Almost as soon as the child was on the mend, Louis himself collapsed, suffering from violent fever, cold sweats, appalling fits of coughing and – most alarmingly – his first major haemorrhage from the lungs. Summoned by the local doctor to nurse him, Fanny at first took Louis to a hotel in Oakland but, the expense proving too great, moved him into her own house. Both she and Louis thought he would die, and it was mid April before he was out of danger. That his terrible journey and months of living on the breadline had ruined his already precarious health is obvious; the true nature of his illness is still a matter of debate.

In the nineteenth century, before X-rays were available as a diagnostic tool, all lung disease that resulted in blood-spitting was classified as 'consumption', or tuberculosis. The local physician who treated Louis during his illness in California diagnosed 'galloping consumption', and

Louis himself believed that he was tubercular. Against the case is the fact that although tuberculosis is highly infectious – the poet John Keats contracted it from his brother, and William Wordsworth's daughter Dora after nursing her cousin – Louis is not thought ever to have passed his illness to anyone else; moreover the chiefs in Samoa, who had first-hand knowledge of the symptoms of the tuberculosis spread among their people by Europeans, were convinced that Louis did not have the disease.

More recently a diagnosis of bronchiectasis, a malfunction of the two branches of the windpipe leading into the lungs, has been suggested as more consistent with Louis's symptoms, and might also explain his unnaturally thin physique – although this has also been attributed to a malfunction of the thyroid. Bronchiectasis, thought to be a consequence of severe whooping-cough, or in some cases to be hereditary, is curable by antibiotics, which were not available until the discovery of penicillin in 1928. In the nineteenth century it was rare for sufferers to live beyond their early forties. There is some evidence too that many patients died from brain abscesses which could rupture and mimic the effect of a fatal stroke. It may, of course, be said that it was all the same in the end, but ironically, if Louis did have brochiectasis, the treatment he was given in the belief that he had TB could only have aggravated his condition, as did the chain smoking which, repulsively to the modern mind, he claimed only to stop for coughing and kissing.

* * *

In November 1874 Louis had written, in a letter to Fanny Sitwell, a list of 'Desiderata' for the future:

I. Good Health
II. 2 to 3 hundred a year
III. *O du leiber Gott, friends!*

It was the cry of a frail young man with limited resources, who had found it difficult to fit in as a schoolboy, and who yearned for intimacy with people who would accept him as one of their own. Six years on the first two items on his wish-list were as far as ever from his grasp, but he did have friends who loved him and who provided him with the kind of brotherhood which matters most to only children: his cousin Bob Stevenson, Charles Baxter, Walter Simpson and James Walter Ferrier from his student days in Edinburgh, and in literary London Sidney Colvin, Fanny Sitwell, William Ernest Henley, Edmund Gosse and Andrew Lang. When he ignored their advice and set off across the Atlantic in pursuit of a dream of his own, it was the London friends who reacted most violently, as if somehow, while they married and had families and pursued their own agenda, Louis ought to have remained as he was – boyish, spritely, entertaining and available – because they liked it that way. There was, however, another reason for their horror. In English academic and literary circles at that time there was a snobbish distaste for everything American; when Colvin and Henley had briefly met Fanny Osbourne in 1876, prejudice had automatically kicked in. Fanny's age, her manners, her smoking, her accent (she pronounced 'Louis' as 'Loo-us') were noted with contempt, although Louis's own broad Scottish accent was, interestingly enough, never held against him.

His friends' disapproval followed him to California. Colvin, who recognised Louis's genius and generally promoted it, complained not only about his choice of American subjects for his essays, but found objections to work that had nothing to do with America. He and Henley both disliked 'The Pavilion on the Links' and 'The Story of a Lie', and when parts of *The Amateur Emigrant* found their way to London, their horror was almost comical. This excellent book, stripped of all the mannerisms and *faux* Bohemianism of *An Inland Voyage* and *Travels with a Donkey* and notable for its balance of compassion and realism, was described by Colvin to Charles Baxter as 'not just bad, but probably unsaleable, quite below his mark ...'. He went on, pompously:

> I don't believe that this [failure to make the most of his talent] will go as long as he lives away from his equals. ... Of course there is always the chance of his settling to some cadging second-rate literary work out there, and if I am not mistaken Mrs O. would certainly not at all object to that result.

The condescension is breathtaking, and it is a relief to discover that such intellectual, and indeed social, snobbery was not entirely a British phenomenon. The Bostonian novelist Henry James later proved every bit as disdainful of his Indiana compatriot, referring to Fanny as 'a poor, barbarous and merely instinctive lady'. It was against this background that Louis, in dedicating *The Amateur Emigrant* to Bob Stevenson, wistfully included 'all in the old country' in 'the greeting of [his] heart'.

1 and 2. Thomas and Margaret Stevenson, parents of Robert Louis Stevenson

3. Photograph of Robert Louis Stevenson aged 3, taken by Edinburgh photographer John Moffat.

4. Robert Louis Stevenson aged about ten.

5. The Stevenson family with Alison Cunningham (right) and two maids.

6. Robert Louis Stevenson as an advocate.

7. Panorama of the city of Edinburgh looking to the west from Calton Hill, from Daniel Wilson's scrapbook (19th century).

8. Fanny Osbourne.

9. Woodcut by Joe Strong, used as frontispiece of *The Silverado Squatters*, of the disused miner's cabin where Robert Louis Stevenson and Fanny spent their honeymoon in 1880.

10. William Ernest Henley (1849-1903).

11. This map was published with the first edition of the novel *Kidnapped* (London: 1886).

12. Long John Silver examines the map of Treasure Island. An illustration by Walter Paget from *Treasure Island*, 1899.

13. Map of Treasure Island, drawn by Robert Louis Stevenson for the first edition of his book – but not the original map he drew for Lloyd in Braemar.

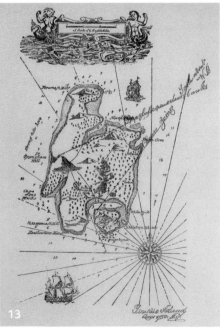

14. At Saranac Lake,
New York State, 1887-88.
Left to right: Valentine
Roche, an unnamed
servant, Lloyd Osbourne,
Fanny Stevenson and
Robert Louis Stevenson.

16. Robert Louis
Stevenson and his family
entertain King Kalakaua
of Hawaii. Left to right:
Lloyd Osbourne, Fanny,
Robert Louis Stevenson
and King Kalakaua.

15. The *Casco*, hired by
Robert Louis Stevenson
for his first voyage in the
Pacific, 1888-89.

17. Robert Louis Stevenson and Fanny visiting Butaritari in 1889.

18. Robert Louis Stevenson and crew members on the bowsprit of the *Equator*.

19. *Equator*, Honolulu, 1889.

20. The cover of *Catriona*, the sequel to *Kidnapped*, published in 1893.

21. Family and servants at *Vailima*, 1892. Left to right: Joe Strong, Mary Carter (Australian maid), Margaret Stevenson, Lloyd Osbourne, Robert Louis Stevenson, Fanny Stevenson, Belle Strong and Austin Strong.

21

22. *Vailima.*
Watercolour by Belle, 1891.

23. Robert Louis Stevenson
by Count Girolamo Nerli,
painted at *Vailima* in 1892.

24. The tomb of 'Tusitala' on
Mount Vaea, Upolu, Western
Samoa. Fanny Stevenson's ashes
were interred beside the body
of Robert Louis Stevenson
after her death in 1914.

He must have believed then that Bob, who had been his friend for longest, would remain so for the rest of their days.

* * *

In Edinburgh, happily, a thaw was underway. It was Sidney Colvin who conveyed to Tom and Maggie that Mrs Osbourne had actually obtained a divorce from her husband, a development which had seemed to them impossible, and a little money from his father began to trickle through to Louis in California. But, just as when Louis had been sent off to Menton by Dr Clark in 1874, it was the news their son was seriously ill in 'a friend's house' in Oakland following a haemorrhage that finally demolished the barrier of hurt and anger between them. Maggie, haunted by the fear that Louis had inherited pulmonary disease from her, wanted to tear off to California immediately, and only the medical advice that such a journey would kill Tom prevented her. In mid April, however, when Louis was just beginning to drag himself back to the land of the living, friendly letters began to arrive from 17 Heriot Row, along with a telegram from Tom with the wonderful injunction: 'Count on 250 pounds annually.' Euphoric and in a forgiving mood, Louis now wished to let all bygones be bygones. A conciliatory letter was despatched to Colvin, telling him the good news, and to Edmund Gosse he wrote: 'Do write, Wegg; and if you are angry with me, bury that damned hatchet straight away and be hanged to you. I shall go to the mountains as soon as the weather clears; on the way thither, I marry myself; then I set up my family altar among the pinewoods, 3000 feet, sir, from the disputatious sea.'

On 19 May 1880 Louis, wearing new false teeth but otherwise, as he ruefully described himself, 'a mere complication of cough and bones, much fitter for an emblem of mortality than a bridegroom', married Fanny Osbourne in San Francisco with only one friend, Dora Williams, as witness. Silver rings were exchanged, because Fanny thought gold too extravagant. Before they adjourned to the Viennese Bakery for lunch, Louis presented the officiating minister not with one of his own books, but with a copy of a religious tract in defence of Christianity, written by his father.

CHAPTER 12

Treasure Island

It was far, indeed, from being my first book, for I am not a novelist alone. But I am well aware that my paymaster, the great public, regards what else I have written with indifference, if not aversion. If it calls upon me at all, it calls on me in the familiar and indelible character; and when I am asked to talk of my first book, no question in the world but what is meant is my first novel.

– Preface to Treasure Island, 1893 –

THE NEWLY-WED STEVENSONS' honeymoon must rank among the most eccentric ever. Louis and Fanny agreed that his recuperation required time away from the choking summer sea fogs which licked around the Oakland cottage, and Louis's first thought was that the Sacramento Valley in north California might suit him well. Fanny, probably guided by Louis's doctor, overruled him; she said that he needed to spend time at a really high altitude, and so, within a few days of the wedding and accompanied by Lloyd and his dog Chuchu, they travelled to the Hot Springs Hotel at Calistoga in the Napa Valley east of San Francisco. Here Louis used a telephone for the first time, but confessed that otherwise he found the Calistoga area 'a land of stage-drivers and highwaymen ... like England a hundred years ago'. Even with the guarantee of £200 a year, the weekly bill of $30 for three was too much to contemplate long-term, and when a local storekeeper suggested that they could live rent free at Silverado, an abandoned mining town high up on the flank of Mount Helena, it was decided to give it a try. In this 'world of wreck and rust, splinters and rolling gravel', windy, unstable, sulphurous and inhabited by enormous rattlesnakes, Louis and his new family attempted to make a temporary home in the only building left on the site, a dilapidated shack once used as a miners' dormitory.

When Louis came to make a book out of the experience in *The*

Silverado Squatters, also published as the third section of *The Amateur Emigrant*, Louis did his best to emphasise the positive, with loving descriptions of the flowers and the view to San Francisco Bay and the beauty of the night sky, and kindly portraits of their few neighbours. But expected supplies did not arrive on time, within two days of their arrival Fanny's efforts at DIY resulted in a smashed thumb, and by the end of the week she and Lloyd both had to be evacuated because of diphtheria. Although a second more lengthy stay was attempted after their recovery, no amount of rhapsodising about freedom and delicious camp-cooking and drinking wine under the stars could conceal the sheer impossibility of sustaining such a life for long.

By the end of July the squatters were back in San Francisco, staying with Joe and Belle Strong, now uneasily reconciled with her mother. Louis, convinced by the 'galloping consumption' diagnosis and beset with intimations of mortality, was feeling an urgent need to get back home, as he confessed to Fanny's brother Jacob Vandegrift: 'I may very well never see next spring. In view of this, I am all the more anxious that [Fanny] should see my father and mother; they are well off, thank God; and even suppose that I die, Fanny will be better off than she has much chance of being otherwise.'

On 7 August, having travelled first class by rail from San Francisco to New York, Louis, Fanny and Lloyd embarked on the SS *City of Chester* as saloon passengers, courtesy of Tom Stevenson, arriving in Liverpool ten days later. Sidney Colvin, on the spur of the moment, decided to go to meet them, and a deliciously gossipy letter to Henley followed:

> They were pleased, and I was glad to have gone, though I am not sure that I should have done so had I known that the old folks were going too. ... I stopped four or five hours and lunched with the united family – old Mrs Stevenson (who looks the fresher of the two), young Mrs Stevenson, old Mr Stevenson, Mr Louis Stevenson, and Sam [Lloyd] – who distinguished himself ... by devouring the most enormous luncheon that ever descended a mortal gullet. It was too soon to tell how [Louis] really was; in the face he looked better than I expected, and improved by his new teeth; but weak and easily fluttered, and so small you never saw, you could put your thumb and finger round his thigh. On the whole he didn't seem to me a bit like a dying man, in spite of everything.

All of which was praising with faint damns and catty in bits, but only when he came to describe 'young Mrs Stevenson' did Colvin really extend his claws.

> It is clear enough that [Louis] likes his new estate so far all right ... but whether you and I will ever get reconciled to the little determined brown face and white teeth and grizzling (for that's what it's up to) grizzling hair, which we are to see beside him in the future, that is another matter.

The following day the Stevensons took the train north to Edinburgh, alighting at Waverley Station, where Louis had given his parents the slip a year before. Now things could not have been more different. Although she had admitted to her cousin that Fanny was not 'the daughter-in-law I have always pictured to myself', Maggie found Fanny easy to like and was warmed by her obvious concern for Louis. Tom, who had gone against his wife's opinion by liking Fanny Sitwell, now concurred with it, and with surprising ease the family of three became a family of five, with Lloyd as an honorary grandson. Together they all set off for a holiday at Strathpeffer where Louis, after his year in America, rediscovered the Scot in himself, looking at the Highland scenery with sharpened eyes. He began to plan a history of the Act of Union between Scotland and England in 1707, and perhaps even had thoughts of settling in Scotland again. If so, the weather soon reminded him sharply of its baneful effect and, on his uncle Dr George Balfour's advice, it was decided that he should spend the coming winter at Davos in Switzerland. Davos was a fashionable and expensive resort with consumptive and nervous patients, due to the presence of Dr Karl Ruedi, a lung specialist who offered an 'Alpine cure'.

Needless to say the promised £200 a year would hardly begin to cover the cost, so once again Tom Stevenson became the family's provider. Despite his previous high-minded pronouncements about supporting himself by writing, Louis seems to have been untroubled by this multiple dependency, perhaps having decided that his invalid status absolved him from any responsibility. For the remaining years of Tom's life, Louis and Fanny got into the habit of spending recklessly, secure in the knowledge that Tom would pick up the bills. This is how Lloyd Osbourne, too, acquired his taste for the high life, which the Stevensons would fund for evermore.

At the Grosvenor Hotel in London, which they reached in October 1880, accompanied by Lloyd and a disruptive Skye terrier, Woggs, given to them as a wedding present by Sir Walter Simpson, Colvin's question to Henley was immediately answered. Louis's friends did not like Fanny, and Fanny hated them. 'It is not good for the mind, or the body either,' she wrote intemperately to Maggie, 'to sit smiling until I feel like a hypocritical Cheshire cat, at Louis's friends, talking stiff nothings with one and another in order for Louis to get a chance with the one he most cares for, and all the time watching the clock and thirsting for their life's blood because they stay so late.' Although part of her fury was doubtless due to anxiety for Louis, she was also jealous and insecure, convinced that under their veneer of good manners the friends despised and resented her. These first impressions, never modified, would cause much distress in the years ahead.

During the long winter at Davos, Dr Ruedi diagnosed Louis as having 'chronic pneumonia ... and a bronchitic tendency' and advised him to stop smoking – advice which of course he ignored. Fanny had an attack of vague illness and was advised to lose weight, prompting Louis to rude jokes about 'butterballs'. He went on planning his book on the Union, which was destined never to see the light of day, and arranged his essays for the collection published in 1881 as *Virginibus Puerisque*, but did little or no new work. The latter part of the stay was darkened by the arrival of Fanny Sitwell and her son; Bertie, who had once been Louis's playfellow at Cockfield Rectory, was in the last stages of tuberculosis. Louis was sympathetic but kept a rather embarrassed distance, and when Bertie died in April he left it to Sidney Colvin to support the twice-bereaved mother. In the same month the Stevensons headed back to Scotland and what, for Louis, would be one of the most creative summers of his life.

*   *   *

At the end of May, accompanied by Maggie, Lloyd and the evilly disposed Woggs, Louis and Fanny travelled north to Kinnaird Cottage, Pitlochry, on which Tom Stevenson had taken a two-month lease. To call the accommodation cramped is an understatement; although it was in a picturesque situation, the cottage had only two main rooms, and the dining-room was so small that the servant had no room to hand round dishes. Visits from Tom, Colvin and Gosse meant even more squeezing up. The rain poured, the wind screamed, and Maggie and Fanny were drenched to the skin; Woggs, who would die at Bournemouth after a vicious dog fight, got in plenty of practice. Only Louis prospered; kept indoors by the weather, he had nothing to do but write. Two of his most powerful short stories, 'Thrawn Janet' (in Scots) and 'The Merry Men', were written that summer, both heavily atmospheric tales in which the Devil of Cummy's stories once again stalked the earth, and both pointers to the distinctively Scottish novelist that Stevenson was yet to become. At Pitlochry too Louis had the bizarre idea – considering how he had sneered his way through university – of applying for the vacant professorship of History and Constitutional Law at Edinburgh University. Despite his obvious lack of qualifications, he seems to have thought that with references from his literary friends and the Stevensons' importance in Edinburgh society, the job was his for the taking. To the deep annoyance of his parents, who also believed their name carried weight, the appointing committee disagreed.

At the end of July, hoping irrationally for better weather further north, the family moved on to Braemar where they took a house known, to Louis's amusement, as 'the late Miss McGregor's cottage'. The rain continued to pour, and Louis and his father began to get on each other's nerves again; there was a row over *The Amateur Emigrant*, which Tom was agitating to have withdrawn because 'I think it not only the worst thing you have ever done, but altogether unworthy of you'. What he meant, of course, was 'unworthy of me', since he was mortified by the prospect of people knowing the squalor his son had endured. Lloyd, bored to distraction, took to papering the walls with pictures made 'with aid of pen and ink and a shilling box of water-colours'. Louis, who tended with Lloyd to take the role of elder brother, sometimes spent the afternoon with him, and so it was, as he recalled in 'My First Book', that

> ... I made a map of an island; it was elaborately and (I thought) beautifully coloured; the shape of it took my fancy beyond expression; it contained harbours that pleased me like sonnets; and, with the unconsciousness of the predestined, I ticketed my performance *Treasure Island*. ... As I pored upon my map of *Treasure Island*, the future characters of the book began to appear there visibly among imaginary woods; and their brown faces and bright weapons peeped out upon me from unexpected quarters, as they passed to

and fro, fighting and hunting treasure, on these few square inches of a flat projection. The next thing I knew, I had some paper before me, and was writing out a list of chapters.

This was the genesis of *Treasure Island*, the most famous 'adventure for boys' ever written. Loved by children for its exciting, cliff-hanging narrative, scenes of horror and vivid sense of character and place, it was also admired by adults for its moral ambiguity, its brilliant portrayal of the anti-hero, the Janus-faced pirate Long John Silver, and its 'heart of darkness' which anticipates Joseph Conrad. Like all great novels it may be read on different levels by different readers, and re-read with new insights throughout the individual reader's life. With the working title *The Sea Cook*, Louis wrote 15 chapters in as many days, reading each one to the family in the afternoon. It became habitual for Lloyd Osbourne in later life to claim a greater role in his stepfather's work than he ever had; this is evidenced by the fact that it was Tom Stevenson, with his long habit of putting himself to sleep by inventing stories of ships, roadside inns, robbers and old sailors who, diverted from squabbling, entered Louis's imagined world with 'all the romance and childishness of his original nature'. When the time came for Billy Bones's sea chest to be broken into, Louis remembered that his father 'must have spent the better part of a day preparing, on the back of a legal envelope, an inventory of its contents ... and the name of "Flint's old ship", the *Walrus*, was given at his particular request'. Fanny, who fancied herself as a literary critic, was unenthusiastic and found the book 'tedious'; only later, when *Treasure Island* became Louis's most famous and lucrative book, did she decide that she had liked it all the time.

It so happened that among the visitors to 'the late Miss McGregor's cottage' that summer was Dr Alexander Japp, a scholar and biographer who had read Louis's essay on Henry David Thoreau and wanted to discuss it with the author. The visit was providential. Japp had been asked by the owner of *Young Folks* magazine to scout for new contributors; as he loved the story of *The Sea Cook*, he took the manuscript away with him when he left. *Young Folks* accepted the story for serialisation, the title was changed to *Treasure Island*, and Louis found himself with writer's block and half the book still to be written. A second spurt of inspiration fortunately occurred when he was on his way back to Davos for a second winter, and writing again at the rate of a chapter a day he completed the book. It was published in book form in 1883, and has

93

never been out of print since. Its enduring power ensured that in the twentieth century it would be transformed into films, radio and television serials, websites and interactive games. The characters of Long John Silver, Blind Pew, Israel Hands and the cabin boy Jim Hawkins would fire the imagination of successive generations, making pirates a perennial theme of parties and fancy-dress parades. In 2007 a Scottish school, Dollar Academy, published its own edition of the book, with haunting new illustrations by Angus Maclean; the *Jolly Roger* flew overhead and a whole year's activities, for five to 18-year-olds, were centred on *Treasure Island*.

* * *

It was with some reluctance that Louis returned to Davos in October, but by now it had become clear to him that he could not tolerate the dark, damp winters of his native land. He disliked the resort, but the clear air of the mountains suited him, and during this second winter he wrote *The Silverado Squatters*, and an essay which would be published later as 'Talk and Talkers', and sketched not only *Prince Otto* but a story called 'The Murder of Red Colin', from which would evolve the first of his great Scottish novels, *Kidnapped*. His essay on Samuel Pepys appeared in the *Cornhill Magazine*, and to his delight he had offers for books from two London publishers. 'Really I ought to make money now,' he wrote to his father who, given the horrendous expense he was incurring, could have been forgiven for scepticism.

The worst problem of the second Davos winter was Fanny who, throughout her marriage, usually followed an illness of Louis's with one of her own. Critics and doctors have had divergent views on why this happened, but most agree that many of Fanny's ailments were psychosomatic. It seems, however, that on this occasion she had a genuine physical problem, which doctors suspected was caused by the passage of a gallstone which had ulcerated her bowel. Her nervous condition – 'brain-fever' was again mentioned – was more probably due to boredom, her inability to get on with servants, a long-distance quarrel with Belle, and a frustrated desire to be the focus of attention. Louis was really ill in November, his cough so severe that he had to swig a mixture of chloral and hashish (cannabis) from a bottle at his side. 'Fanny and I both in bed together,' he wrote dolefully to Charles Baxter, 'with a hired sick nurse; Woggs wailing with an abscess in his ear; and Sam (Lloyd) with his hand in a splint.' But Fanny's departure for a month of medical treatment in Zurich and Berne, taking Lloyd with her, did not suit Louis either; he was lonely, and the week before Christmas he journeyed to Berne to fetch them back. Maggie and Tom must have been appalled by the letter he wrote on Boxing Day:

> Yesterday ... we finished this eventful journey by a drive in an *open* sleigh ... seven hours on end, through whole forests of Christmas trees. The cold was beyond belief; I have often suffered less at a dentist's. ... My only terror was that Fanny should ask for brandy or laudanum or something. So awful was the thought of putting my hands out, that I half thought I would refuse.

He hastened to add that 'none of us are a penny the worse', but both he and Fanny were soon back in bed. In the early months of 1882 Louis's health gradually improved, but until April 1882, when they left Davos for good, his letters catalogued despairingly the ups and downs in Fanny's mysterious condition. 'I wish to God,' he wrote to Colvin, 'I or anyone knew what was the matter with my wife.'

* * *

In the month of their departure, the first part of Louis's essay 'Talk and Talkers' was published in the *Cornhill Magazine*. In it Louis wrote of his friends under disguised names; Henley became 'Burly', Bob Stevenson 'Spring-Heel'd Jack', Fleeming Jenkin 'Cockshot', Gosse 'Purcel' and Simpson 'Athelred'. If the essay was intended to flatter, it misfired; those who were not included were huffy, some who were did not recognise themselves, and those who did took umbrage at the way they had been depicted. The reception of the essay must have brought home to Louis how the easy fellowship of old was cracking up, as other people's lives moved on in his absence. Most of his treasured relationships had some way to run, but with Bob and Walter Simpson married, Charles Baxter a recently bereaved father, his Edinburgh friend James Walter Ferrier dying of alcoholism and Fanny Sitwell reduced to a slightly embarrassing memory, mutability was in the air. The gradual loosening of ties could only make it easier, when the time came, to slip the knots altogether.

CHAPTER 13

Skerryvore

Marriage is one long conversation, chequered by disputes. The disputes are valueless; but they ingrain the difference; the heroic heart of woman prompting her at once to nail her colours to the mast. But in the intervals, almost unconsciously and with no desire to shine, the whole material of life is turned over and over, ideas are struck out and shared, the two persons more and more adapt their notions one to suit another, and in process of time, without sound or trumpet, they conduct each other into new worlds of thought.

– 'Talk and Talkers', 1882 –

AT HIS FINAL appointment with Dr Ruedi, Louis had received the pleasing news that his lungs were 'splendid', but also a warning that in future he should live in the south of France, within 15 miles of the sea. The next three years of his life were spent trying to find a suitable place to settle; Nice, Saint Marcel near Marseilles and Royat were tried and found wanting, and only a chalet named 'La Solitude' at Hyères-les-Palmiers near Toulon was remembered by Louis as a place where he had been happy. Periods of prostrating illness alternated with spells of frantic literary activity; *Prince Otto*, a tale of love and court intrigue in an imaginary German state, and *The Black Arrow*, an adventure story set during the English Wars of the Roses, were both completed at this time. Louis thought that *Prince Otto* was a work of some stature and *The Black Arrow* 'mere tushery', a judgement reversed by posterity. Also written at this difficult time were the poems first called *Penny Whistles*, then *A Child's Garden of Verses*. The universality of the poems, with their mixture of joy and melancholy, light and shade, swiftly turned them into a classic, while their florid dedication to the old nurse who had long since been consigned to a walk-on part in Louis's adult life gave Cummy a gift of fame which she would not be slow to exploit.

The French interlude came to an abrupt end in January 1884 when, after a rollicking and, to Fanny's deep disapproval, bibulous visit from Henley and Baxter, Louis became so ill with an infection of his lungs and kidneys that Fanny was warned that he might not survive. Furious that Henley and Baxter had, she alleged, caused her husband's collapse, Fanny cabled two of his other friends, Bob Stevenson and Walter Simpson, to come and help out. When they declined, she added them to her growing list of hate figures. Even Louis's parents did not escape censure; their first reaction had been to suggest that the illness was 'just nerves', then, belatedly realising their mistake, to panic and swamp both Fanny and Louis's doctor with terrified telegrams. There were many setbacks over the next few months, including more haemorrhages and a severe recurrence of the ophthalmia which had afflicted Louis in Paris before his marriage, but gradually he began to recover. It was clear, however, that living in the south of France gave no guarantee of good health, and a summer outbreak of cholera in Marseilles sent the Stevensons scuttling back to England. It would have broken Louis's heart to know that he would never see the Mediterranean again.

Louis and Fanny met Tom and Maggie at Richmond-on-Thames. Louis was too exhausted to go further, so on 4 July Fanny and her parents-in-law went up to London without him. The occasion was the premiere of *Deacon Brodie* at The Prince's Theatre, with Henley's younger brother Edward in the title role. Surprisingly this dire piece was reasonably well reviewed. When he had rested, Louis consulted doctors, some of whom said that he might live quite healthily on the south coast of England, while others contradicted this opinion. He himself decided to give it a try, principally because at Richmond he had been so alarmed by the sight of his father. It was not only that Tom, who two years before had complained robustly to Dr Japp about the impudence of an Aberdeen cab driver in referring to him as 'an old gentleman', had aged suddenly; there were disturbing signs that mentally he was not quite the man he had been. Louis felt that for both his parents' sakes he should be as close as possible, and when Fanny suggested a stay at Bournemouth, since the 1840s a spa town much favoured by invalids with chest problems, he agreed. That Lloyd was in Bournemouth being tutored for university entrance was a bonus for Fanny, although it had already been decided that in the autumn he would move to Edinburgh to study engineering. At this point, Lloyd had his eye on the Stevenson family business.

After a short spell in lodgings, a house, Bonallie Tower, was rented in an leafy area of the town, and almost immediately Louis's friends, oblivious of having given offence to Fanny only months earlier, began to pile in to visit. Among the first was Henley, high as a kite after the production of *Deacon Brodie*, lurching about on his crutch and noisily full of ideas for new plays to make them rich. While Fanny gritted her teeth and doled out small drinks, he and Louis set to work on *Beau Austin*, a conventional piece about young women looking for husbands in Georgian Tunbridge Wells, and *Admiral Guinea*, a melodrama featuring the terrifying beggar Blind Pew, which shamelessly revisited the territory of *Treasure Island*. If the toy theatres of Skelt had any lasting influence on the work of Robert Louis Stevenson, it was surely on these crude, two-dimensional plays. Henley was much at Bournemouth during the following months, braving Fanny's rudeness and interference in the last great flush of friendship and collaboration.

Although the mild winter climate of Bournemouth did not noticeably improve Louis's health, he and Fanny decided to stay. In May 1885, in a gesture of personal generosity to Fanny, though certainly also in the hope of tying the vagabond couple down, Tom Stevenson bought his daughter-in-law a house, a villa of yellow brick and blue slate above the chalk cliffs on the outskirts of Westbourne. Its unimaginative name, 'Sea View', was changed by Louis to 'Skerryvore', in honour of his uncle Alan Stevenson's *magnum opus,* and with an additional gift of £500 from Tom, Fanny set about furnishing the house in her own style. With blue walls, yellow damask throws, oak boxes and Japanese vases on the chimney-piece, the sitting-room was a far cry from the usual stifling and cluttered Victorian parlour; while in the garden Fanny laid out flower-beds and grew un-Victorian crops like raspberries, sweetcorn, lettuces and tomatoes. Sadly, what might have been a happy time was shadowed both by Louis's continuing frailty and by Tom Stevenson's descent into senility, which was more obvious every time the parents came to stay.

Louis's relationship with his father was more peaceful than of yore, for all that Tom's decline had not stifled his outspoken criticism. Unfortunately Fanny, whose anxiety for Louis's health was the more acceptable face of extreme possessiveness, found it less easy than in the early days of marriage to get on with Maggie, who resented being ordered not to sneeze near her son. Whether the English weather was to blame, or whether Fanny, who seems to have had an understanding of infection ahead of her time, insisted on making him more reclusive than he needed to be, Louis rarely ventured further than the garden at

Skerryvore. Fortunately friends came to him; not only his old London comrades, but also neighbours. An undistinguished young woman named Adelaide Boodle called with her mother, infiltrated the household and lived to publish an effusive myth-promoting tribute, *RLS and his Sine Qua Non*, in 1926. Sir Percy Florence Shelley, son of the poet Percy Bysshe Shelley and Mary Shelley of *Frankenstein* fame, provided a literary link with the past; there were also two distinguished American visitors, the artist John Singer Sargent and the novelist Henry James, who was in Bournemouth visiting his peripatetic invalid sister Alice.

Sargent's portrait of Louis prowling the dining-room like a skeleton in a black coat and pale trousers, with Fanny sitting ghostlike on the sideline in a chair, is the most disturbing and elusive image of this often portrayed man, justifying Sargent's remark that Stevenson was 'the most intense creature I had ever met'. But it was Henry James who became a life-long friend; the patrician Bostonian observer of life, as different from Stevenson as chalk from cheese, got into the habit of dropping in after dinner; Louis's grandfather's chair, in which Fanny sat in the Sargent portrait, was renamed 'Henry James's chair', and Louis celebrated their friendship in verse:

Now with an outlandish grace
To the sparkling fire I face
In the blue room at Skerryvore;
And I wait until the door
Open, and the Prince of Men,
Henry James shall come again.

– 'The Mirror Speaks' –

In spite of the pleasure James's company gave him, Louis was in a dark mood throughout 1885. His father's painful and prolonged decline, his mother's natural anxiety and his own ill health weighed on him, and the work he produced, the short stories 'Markheim' and 'Olalla', with their different versions of souls in torment, show his growing preoccupation with sin, retribution and the improbability, as he saw it, of redemption. 'Olalla', a bloody and vampiric tale set in early nineteenth-century Spain, is perhaps too lush and melodramatic for modern taste, but the sparer 'Markheim' frightens through its brooding atmosphere and ambivalence. The unambiguous Devil of 'Thrawn Janet' and 'The Merry Men' is here replaced by a ghostly visitor, whose

99

role as devil or angel is never resolved, to Markheim who murdered an antique dealer on Christmas Day. To this period too belong the lines:

The look of Death is both severe and mild,
And all the words of Death are grave and sweet;
He holds ajar the door of his retreat;
The hermitage of life, it may be styled. …

– New Poems LXVII *–*

During the second part of the year, Louis was occupied in a sad task; his old mentor Fleeming Jenkin had died suddenly at the age of 53, reinforcing Louis's awareness of the fragility of life. Asked by Anne Jenkin to write her husband's biography, he felt unable to refuse, although he had to lay aside the first draft of *Kidnapped* to do so. And it was his inability, in the midst of so much else, to sustain his enthusiasm for the plays which still meant so much to Henley that caused the first crack in what, until then, had been the most jovial and supportive relationship of both their lives.

In the summer a holiday on Dartmoor was ventured, in the company of Lloyd and Katharine de Mattos. It started with a pleasant visit to fellow-novelist Thomas Hardy in Dorchester, but had to be abandoned when Louis became ill at Exeter, spending several dreary weeks in a hotel before he was able to travel home. Confined to bed at Skerryvore, pumped full of laudanum and again beset with vivid nightmares, he wrote at great speed what was to become an overnight sensation and one of his best known works. It also occasioned one of the marital disputes which 'chequered' the 'conversation' of the Stevenson marriage, though not one to be lightly dismissed.

Strange Case of Dr Jekyll and Mr Hyde tells how Dr Jekyll, a London physician interested in the good and evil aspects of his own personality, speculates on the advantage of being able to separate the two. In his laboratory he experiments with a drug which proves able to transfer his evil instincts into 'Mr Hyde', a sinister creature who arouses horror in all who encounter him. Jekyll's ability to control Hyde at first gives him a false sense of security; too late he realises that his evil *alter ego* is inexorably getting the upper hand. When the drug loses its power to restore Jekyll to his own body and he is about to be arrested for a foul murder committed by Hyde, he commits suicide.

There were many 'shilling shockers' published in the late nineteenth century, containing a similar mix of sensation and horror. What makes *Strange Case of Dr Jekyll and Mr Hyde* outstanding, apart from the quality of its writing, is not only its original twist on the age-old war between good and evil, but the way it plugs uncannily into modern pre-occupations: the multi-faceted nature of the human psyche, the terror of loss of identity, and the perils of addiction. Despite its London setting, it is as Scottish a story as its great forerunner, James Hogg's *The Private Memoirs and Confessions of A Justified Sinner*, published in 1824. A belief in the supernatural was embedded in the national consciousness, emerging in countless myths and folk tales, while it was the uncompromising split in the Calvinist vision between good and evil, the saved and the damned, that had led the adult Stevenson to reject the version of Christianity in which he had been reared. Whatever its supposed location, *Strange Case of Dr Jekyll and Mr Hyde* translates most convincingly to divided Edinburgh, home of Deacon Brodie – the town of respectability and vice, wealth and poverty which fascinated and repelled Louis in equal measure.

In his essay 'Talk and Talkers' Louis had paid generous tribute to his marriage to Fanny, and the way they 'struck out and shared' ideas. No doubt this had encouraged Fanny, who had literary ambitions of her own, to see his writing as a joint enterprise; certainly she had got into the habit of criticising every line Louis wrote and had even become a collaborator, acting, she said complacently, as Scheherazade to his Sultan in the composition of *More New Arabian Nights*. Louis, however, had always claimed that the inspiration for his stories came from dreams, and spoke of the 'Brownies' who delved to bring his visions into the light of his waking mind. The story (according to Fanny and later, with minor variations to Lloyd) was that *Strange Case of Dr Jekyll and Mr Hyde* was dream-inspired, but that Fanny, invited to criticise the first draft, had, with reluctance, felt obliged to say that Louis had completely missed the point of his own story. It was, she told him, 'a great moral allegory that the dream was obscuring', which caused Louis to have a mega tantrum and burn the manuscript in his bedroom grate. Fortunately, as Fanny sat 'desolate before the fire', Louis saw the light and came hurrying downstairs crying, 'You are right! I have absolutely missed the allegory, which is the whole point of it'. Setting to work immediately, he rewrote the story in three days, along the lines that Fanny had suggested – thus enabling her to claim responsibility for the psychological and moral strength of one of her husband's greatest works.

This self-serving tale, which first surfaced in the 1901 biography of Stevenson commissioned by Fanny and Lloyd, has not found favour with modern critics, who point out that a writer of Stevenson's intelligence and sophistication would scarcely have missed the point of the allegory in his own story. The most plausible explanation for the burning and rewriting is that Louis had originally made Hyde's 'disgraceful pleasures' sexually explicit, and that what Fanny feared was damage to his reputation at a time when the subject was taboo. Louis's resentment was expressed in a rarely disloyal letter to Henley around this time: 'I got my little finger into a steam press called the Vandegrifter (patent) and my whole body and soul had to go through after it. I came out as limp as a lady's novel, but the Vandegrifter suffered in the process, and is fairly knocked about.' Yet in the prim climate of the 1880s, Fanny may have had a valid point which Louis, however reluctantly, accepted, and that is why the author who stood every other convention of Victorian writing on its head seemed to be more comfortable with male characters. It was not until he got to the South Seas, at the very end of his life, that Louis found himself able to write about sex openly.

*   *   *

The year 1886 was one of illness at Skerryvore. Fanny, without the pleasure of creating a new home which had sustained her the previous year, again became depressed and sickly, while Louis spent almost all his time in bed, suffering minor episodes of the haemorrhaging which he referred to as 'Bluidy Jack'. In some ways this was the nadir of his life, the only point at which this active, gregarious man withdrew into the seclusion of his bedroom, living, as he said later, 'like a weevil in a biscuit'. His letters home contain constant bulletins about his health and Fanny's, and can have done nothing to alleviate Maggie's stress as she tried to cope with Tom's inexorable mental decline. Louis tried to help by giving her a break; in April 1886 he accompanied his father for a week to a hydropathic hotel at Matlock Wells in Derbyshire, where Tom's violent mood-swings led inevitably to a half humorous comparison with Jekyll and Hyde. Yet his father's plight moved Louis deeply, and set him thinking again about his failure to emulate the 'lighthouse Stevensons'; on his return to Bournemouth he composed lines that can be read as an elegy for his father, and also his own his last word on the subject:

Say not of me that weakly I declined
The labours of my sires, and fled the sea,
The towers we founded and the lamps we lit,
To play at home with paper like a child.
But rather say: in the afternoon of time
A strenuous family dusted from its hands
The sand of granite, and beholding far
Along the sounding coasts its pyramids
And tall memorials catch the dying sun,
Smiled well content, and to this childish task
Around the fire addressed its evening hours.

            – 'Say not of me that weakly I declined' –

A temporary escape from the bouts of 'Bluidy Jack' and sad reminiscence came in August when, with Fanny away trying a Swedish 'cure' for rheumatism, Louis went first to London, where he met Robert Browning and the painter Sir Edward Burne-Jones, and joined the gallery of writers sketched by William Blake Richmond. He was, he wrote to his mother, 'enjoying himself to the nines', and went on with Henley to Paris, where he had lunch with the sculptor Auguste Rodin and visited his studio.

Back home there was trouble with Lloyd, whose poor eyesight had been cited as a reason for not sitting engineering exams at Edinburgh University. Both he and Fanny were convinced that he was going blind, although actually there was nothing wrong that a pair of spectacles and a cruise to the West Indies could not cure. By the spring of 1886 Lloyd had decided that engineering was too much hard work, and had abandoned his studies to become a 'professional writer', which in effect meant that he would be a burden on his stepfather's purse for the rest of his days. Louis's connivance remains a mystery; it is clear that a genuinely engaging little boy had grown up idle, snobbish, mercenary and manipulative, but until the last days of his life Louis could see no wrong in Lloyd.

For all its problems and unhappiness, however, 1886 was among Louis's most productive. As well as *Strange Case of Dr Jekyll and Mr Hyde*, it was the year of *Kidnapped*, the first of the great Scottish novels which he seemed only able to write in exile. The tale of a boy tricked out of his inheritance by his wicked uncle and propelled into wild Highland adventures after being kidnapped on a ship bound for America, had every element likely to recommend it to its original readers, the sub-scribers to *Young Folks* magazine – a rattling pace, sword fights, ship-wreck, a brutal murder and a flight over wild Highland moors and mountains – but, as Henry James noted on receiving his copy, it was merely a pretence of Louis's that he wrote 'for boys'. The brilliance of *Kidnapped* is in its masterly study of division in a society riven as much by regional differences of temperament as by the eighteenth-century Jacobite Risings that had brought them into such sharp focus. The boy narrator David Balfour, representative of the cautious, decent but phlegmatic type of the Lowland Scot, is drawn in sharp contrast to the flamboyant Highland adventurer Alan Breck Stewart, whose alleged involvement in the notorious murder in Appin of Red Colin Campbell, factor and kinsman of the Hanoverian Duke of Argyll, lies at the heart of the narrative. There is no doubting where the author's sympathies lay: with the Jacobites against the Hanoverians, with the scenic Highlands against the flat Lowlands, and with the proud clans who 'came out with Prince Charlie' in 1745 against the dour, unadventurous Lowland families who stayed loyal to the London government and the royal house of Hanover. In his dedication to Charles Baxter, Louis admitted 'how little he was touched by the desire for accuracy', and indeed histor-ically the story is very inaccurate indeed. But it speaks much of the way that *Kidnapped* has influenced our self-perception that many Scots, past and present, know and prefer Stevenson's romantic version of events to the more prosaic and ambivalent truth.

CHAPTER 14

Breaking Circles

An open cab, with a man and a woman in it, seated side by side, and leaning back, the rest of the cab piled high with rather untidy luggage – came slowly towards us, westward, along Princes Street. It was evidently carrying travellers to the railway station. As it passed us, out onto the broad roadway ... a slender, loose-garbed figure stood up in the cab and waved a wide-brimmed hat.
'Good-bye!' he called to us. 'Good-bye!'

– Flora Masson, in *I Can Remember Robert Louis Stevenson*, 1922 –

ON HIS LAST visit to London, shortly before his death, Tom Stevenson called on an old friend, the Kincardine-on-Forth born chemist Sir James Dewar, inventor of the vacuum flask. Years before, when Louis announced his intention to become a writer, Dewar had offended Tom by taking Louis's side, betting cheerfully that in ten years' time he would earn more by writing than he would ever have done by joining the family firm. Tom had been in no mood for levity, but now, infirm and aware of approaching death, he had come to make up: 'I cudna be in London without coming to shake your hand and confess that you were richt after all about Louis, and I was wrong.' It is to be hoped that Louis heard of this meeting, and knew that at long last he had actually managed to please his father.

On 4 May 1887 Louis received news at Skerryvore that his father was critically ill. He and Fanny travelled immediately to Edinburgh, arriving at 17 Heriot Row before Tom died, but too late to be recognised. Instead of his father Louis found, as he wrote later:

A something in his likeness. 'Look!' said one,
Unkindly kind, 'look up, it is your boy!'
And the dread changeling gazed on me in vain.

– 'The Last Sight' –

Louis made arrangements for the funeral, the largest ever remembered in Edinburgh for a private citizen, with 300 invited guests and a procession of 50 carriages. Louis, Lloyd and Bob, who had made peace with his uncle long ago, received the guests, but Louis, who was suffering from jaundice as well as 'Bluidy Jack', was too ill to attend the interment in the New Calton Burying Ground. On a cold, squally May day, Tom was laid to rest with Bob as chief mourner, leaving Maggie, Louis and Fanny to plan a future without him.

When the will was read, it was found that Tom had left £3000 to Louis and £2000 to Maggie, who was also to receive the life interest on the remaining estate of £26,000. After her death the remainder of the inheritance was to pass to Louis, and after him to Fanny and Lloyd; Louis was also enjoined to help Bob Stevenson and Katharine de Mattos. Since Louis would predecease his mother, it was the Osbournes who would be the ultimate beneficiaries of Tom's careful husbandry. Meanwhile Louis found himself comfortably off, though not as fabulously wealthy as his friends imagined.

During the three weeks that Louis and Fanny spent at 17 Heriot Row, it became clear that Maggie had had enough of caring for her senile husband in a house heavy with memories. 'Old Mrs Stevenson', who had been brought up on travellers' tales, was only 58 and ready for adventure. Louis was as keen to escape Skerryvore as his mother was to escape Heriot Row, and when it was suggested by Louis's physician uncle that the dry climate of Colorado would suit him, Maggie said that she would finance an extended holiday for herself, Louis, Fanny, Lloyd and a French maid Valentine Roch who had come to Bournemouth with Fanny from Hyères. Louis left Edinburgh on 31 May. He was unaware, as he waved to Flora Masson from the station-bound cab in Princes Street, that he was saying goodbye to his native city for the last time.

While Maggie said her farewells and closed up 17 Heriot Row, Louis and Fanny returned to Bournemouth to let Skerryvore. Fanny may have been sorry to leave her pretty sitting-room and garden, but neither she nor Louis would miss the perpetual sickness and marital rows that had blighted their time there. On August 22 the travelling party met at the London Docks and went on board the SS *Ludgate Hill*, waving to the crowd of well-wishers who had come to see them off.

* * *

The voyage across the Atlantic was not without comedy, though it could not have seemed so funny at the time. At Le Havre, the last port of call before New York, the Stevensons were amazed to discover, as a consignment of apes destined for American zoos and a hundred horses were led on board, that they were not on a cruise liner but on a cattle-boat. Out in the Atlantic the wind began to howl and the sea to rise, making the furniture in the cabins break loose and roll across the floor. Fanny, Lloyd and Valentine were all prostrate with seasickness, their suffering intensified by the fact that, as the ship rode the 40-foot waves, the doleful faces of the horses kept appearing and disappearing outside the window. Maggie was serene, her worst criticism being that 'the strong stable smell' was 'not quite the fine sea air that we expected to blow in at our port-hole'. Louis, who loved the sea at any time, was in his element. When he wasn't correcting the proofs of *Memories and Portraits*, he jinked about merrily on deck, making friends with the apes, plying the seasick with the champagne which was Henry James's parting present, and chatting to everyone. Although he inevitably caught a cold, the euphoria of escape lasted all the way to New York, where his arrival proved unimaginably different from his desolate disembarkation from the SS *Devonia* in 1879.

The Stevensons knew that they were to be the guests of Charles and Elizabeth Fairchild, wealthy admirers of Louis's work and friends of John Singer Sargent, who had brought Charles to visit them in Bournemouth. What they did not know was the runaway success in the United States of *Dr Jekyll and Mr Hyde* – unsurprisingly, since it appeared mostly in 'pirated' editions for which the author was unpaid. So there was no preparation, as the travellers disembarked rather dishevelled from the cattle-boat, for the discovery of a welcoming party consisting of E. L. Burlingame, editor of *Scribner's Magazine*, a reporter from the *New York Herald* and Louis's old Barbizon friend Will Low, who brought the amazing news that a stage adaptation of *Dr Jekyll and Mr Hyde* was about to open in New York. A carriage, sent by the Fairchilds, was waiting to whisk the celebrity and his party off to the Victoria Hotel, where Maggie noted with satisfaction that their luxury suite was the one reserved for 'foreign swells'. More reporters turned up at the hotel in the evening to interview Louis who, despite his reputation at home as a bit of a show-off, was fazed by all the attention. 'My reception here,' he told Colvin, 'was idiotic to the last degree; if Jesus Christ came, they would make less fuss.' The following day, still suffering from the cold he had caught on board ship, he travelled to the Fairchilds' mansion at Newport, Rhode Island. There he took to his bed, incurring the displeasure of the Fairchilds' daughter, who remembered him as a dirty, peculiar, shabby man who smoked too much and burned holes in the sheets.

Back in New York a fortnight later, Louis spent time with Will Low and posed for the sculptor Augustus Saint-Gaudens, who produced a medallion showing the author in bed with his books. (A copy of this work was made by Saint-Gaudens for the memorial to Robert Louis Stevenson unveiled in St Giles Cathedral, Edinburgh in 1904, the only alteration, in deference to the sensibilities of the Kirk, being the replacement of the cigarette in the original with a pen.) He also did business with Edward Burlingame of *Scribner's Magazine* and the publisher Sam McClure who owned the New York *Sun*, amazed by the amount of money they were offering but relieved that his immediate future seemed financially secure.

The only remaining problem was where the family would spend the winter. Colorado had ceased to appeal, so Fanny and Lloyd had gone off to reconnoitre the Adirondacks in upstate New York. The advantages were the same as at Davos, cold mountain winters and the proximity of a TB specialist, Dr Edward Livingstone Trudeau; an additional advantage was that Saranac Lake, where the doctor's clinic was situated, was not a busy resort. Shell-shocked by his reception in New York, Louis was thankful to get away to the white wooden cottage which Fanny had found; it belonged to a mountain guide named Baker, who moved with his wife and two daughters into the back rooms to accommodate his new tenants. Here Louis settled happily, enjoying the spectacular autumn colours and the views of the river as he walked among hills that reminded him of the Highlands. He began to work on the essays he had been commissioned to write for *Scribner's Magazine*, completing in less than a fortnight 'A Chapter on Dreams' and 'The Lantern Bearers'. Although he disliked Dr Trudeau, whose experiments on live animals he found distasteful, Louis was encouraged by the doctor's assurance that he could find no trace of active tuberculosis in his lungs, and began to throw off the invalid's habits of mind and body that had sucked the life out of him in Bournemouth. This was as well, since he was about to experience the most uncomfortable months of his life.

Snow began to fall in early November over Lake Saranac, and the wooden walls of Baker's Cottage, which Louis described as 'our wind-beleaguered hill-top hat-box of a house', did little to keep out the searing cold. Fanny, on her way back from a lengthy visit to her family in Indiana, took a detour by Montreal to buy them all buffalo-skin coats, boots and furry hats, but by December the frost was so intense that ink solidified in the inkwells, Valentine woke to find her handkerchief frozen under her pillow and Louis got frostbite in bed. The family huddled round the stove, trying in vain to keep warm while icy draughts circulated through the poorly insulated rooms. With Fanny ill and Lloyd grumpy, only Louis and his mother remained upbeat and uncomplaining. Will Low, the artist who published his memoirs *A Chronicle of Friendships 1873-1900* in 1908, would remember Maggie Stevenson with admiration: 'She had a keen sense of humour, and her conversation, without any pretension to brilliancy, for one of her most charming traits was a modest assumption of surprise that she should be the mother of so brilliant a son, was always interesting.' At Saranac Lake this unlikely pioneer woman must already have been remembering her sedate Edinburgh life as if it were a dream.

Everyone in the family was busy writing; Maggie long letters to her family at home, Lloyd a comic novel called 'The Finsbury Tontine' (published, after much revision by Louis, as *The Wrong Box*) and Fanny a short story titled 'The Nixie' which, through Louis's influence, she managed to sell to *Scribner's Magazine*. Louis, his twelve contracted essays completed, had started on the novel which is arguably the finest of his completed works, *The Master of Ballantrae*. Explaining how the book was conceived, Louis later wrote:

> I was walking one night on the verandah of a small house in which I lived, outside the hamlet of Saranac. It was winter; the night was very dark; the air extraordinarily clear and cold, and sweet with the purity of forests. From a good way below, the river was to be heard contending with ice and boulders: a few lights appeared, scattered unevenly among the darkness, but so far away as not to lessen the sense of isolation. For the making of a story, here were fine conditions. I was besides moved with the spirit of emulation, having just finished my fourth reading of [Captain Marryat's] *The Phantom Ship*. 'Come,' I said to my engine, 'let us make a tale, a story of many years and many countries, of the sea and the land, savagery and civilisation.' ... There cropped up in my memory a singular case of a buried and resuscitated fakir, which I had often been told

by an uncle of mine, then lately dead, Inspector-General John Balfour.'

The reference to Captain Frederick Marryat (1792-1848), now chiefly remembered for children's books like *Masterman Ready* and *Children of the New Forest*, should not be taken to suggest that, like its predecessors, *The Master of Ballantrae* was conceived as a story for boys. It is a book of adult preoccupation, a tragedy concerned with the clash of good and evil in the human personality, and the split, already, though perhaps less subtly, treated in *Kidnapped*, between Jacobite and Calvinist traits in Scottish life. More than any other of Stevenson's novels, it owes a debt to Sir Walter Scott in its language and structure, though Scott's characters tend to be more sympathetic than the charismatic but diabolic James Durie, the eponymous Master, and his put-upon but ultimately discreditable younger brother Henry. Told mostly through the eyes of the steward Ephraim Mackellar, *The Master of Ballantrae* tells the tragic tale of two brothers locked in mutual hatred, who in 1745 decide by the toss of a coin which will go out to fight for the Jacobite cause and which will sit tight at home for the Hanoverian – a prudent hedging of bets in these turbulent times. The Master leaves home and, after long absence in India and America, returns to find that his brother has assumed his place as heir to the lordship of Durrisdeer and married his fiancée. This is the provocation for a bitter duel and a long campaign of hatred and revenge that will carry these two, complex mirror-images of each other, across the Atlantic and through the wilderness, until they are laid together in the same grave. Stevenson has often been accused of failing to make the endings of his novels as powerful as their beginnings, and certainly the conclusion, inspired by Dr Balfour's story of the resuscitated fakir, requires considerable suspension of disbelief. But the hatred and sense of doom that permeate the book make it as chill in the memory as the winter night at Saranac when Louis first began to imagine it.

* * *

In April the Stevensons moved out of their winter quarters, first to New York and then to a quieter inn on the Manasquan river in New Jersey, found for them by the ever helpful Will Low. Here Louis received an unexpected letter from his friend of twelve years, W. E. Henley, who had written:

I read *The Nixie* with considerable amazement. It's Katharine's; surely it's Katharine's? There are even reminiscences of phrases and imagery; parallel incidents – *que sais-je*? It is also better focused, no doubt; but I don't think it has lost as much (at least) as it has gained; and why there wasn't a double signature is what I've not been able to understand.

'The Nixie' was, of course, the short story which Fanny had written during the winter at Saranac, and sold to *Scribner's Magazine*, and what Henley was suggesting was that she had appropriated it from its original author, Katharine de Mattos, and had passed it off as her own. There was certainly some foundation for this; an idea of Katharine's for a story about a young man's meeting on a train with a mysterious young woman who was in fact an escaped lunatic, had been discussed the previous year in the Henleys' house and in the presence of Louis and Fanny. Fanny, never slow to give literary advice, had immediately suggested 'improve ments', including the re-casting of the young woman as a water-sprite, which Katharine had, at the time, rejected. According to the Stevensons, however, after failing to get her own version of the story published, she had yielded to persuasion and agreed that Fanny could use her material. What muddies the water is that Katharine never actually endorsed this claim, and one is left with the impression that if it is true, the persuasion must have been very heavy-handed indeed.

Whatever the truth, Louis responded with an explosion of outrage: 'I write with indescribable difficulty; and if not with perfect temper, you are to remember how very rarely a husband is expected to receive such accusations against his wife …'. Such were the opening rounds of a bitter quarrel, kept at fever pitch by Fanny, who reacted to the accusation of plagiarism with hysteria verging on mental collapse. Louis was no better; he was sleepless, took opium, had nightmares, fired off angry letters to the hapless Charles Baxter, refused Henley's apology and 'regretted not having died at Hyères'. The sad truth, however, was that Henley's accusing letter only ignited a fuse that had been smouldering for some time.

Louis's comradely affection for his big, boisterous friend had been cooling over a period, affected by Fanny's ill-concealed animosity and the failure of the plays, including the latest, *Macaire*, on which he felt he had wasted valuable time. He also had an aggrieved sense that Henley, Katharine and Bob – who naturally sided with his sister – had ganged up against him and Fanny, and were not grateful enough for money he had been doling out to them since long before he was able to afford it. Henley, who cannot have been entirely flattered to be told by Louis that he had inspired the morally ambiguous one-legged pirate Long John Silver in *Treasure Island*, had perhaps belatedly noticed that he was being patronised; certainly he blamed Louis's lack of enthusiasm for the plays' failure and felt jealous of Louis's American celebrity. Resentful of handouts which he needed, but which underscored his own lack of earning capacity, he was a man in pain who was spoiling for a fight. Bob and Katharine, neither enjoying conspicuous success in life, felt humiliated by the carefully calculated generosity of their cousin, shelling out funds to which, as Alan Stevenson's children, they doubtless felt they had a right. It was sour grapes all round, and the breaking of a circle which Louis had once regarded almost as sacred as the family circle broken only months before. The result was to draw him ever more closely into the family circle of the Osbournes, which in future he would regard as his own.

* * *

The Stevensons had left Edinburgh and Bournemouth intending to return for the summer months, but now, especially with the prospect of having to conduct the war with those Fanny called 'the Shepherd's Bush gang' at close quarters, the idea seemed ever less appealing. Louis, who had been free of 'Bluidy Jack' all winter at Saranac Lake, particularly disliked the thought of being bedridden again at Skerryvore; it was clear to him by now that he only felt really well in the mountains or at sea, and he began to discuss with his mother the possibility of extending their holiday by taking a Pacific cruise. Maggie, who had loved America and had no burning desire to return to stuffy Edinburgh, was delighted, and offered to put up half the cost of hiring a yacht. She and Louis would each contribute £1000, Louis comforting himself with the thought of $10,000 which Sam McClure was offering for a series of letters from the Pacific. Fanny, who had gone to California to visit family and have treatment for what she mistakenly thought was throat cancer, was commissioned to find a suitable vessel, and in May Louis, who was still in New Jersey, received an excited cable: 'Can secure splendid sea-going schooner-yacht *Casco* for $750 a month. ... Reply immediately, Fanny.' 'Blessed girl,' Louis cabled back, 'take the yacht and expect us in ten days.'

This was overly optimistic; the overland journey from Manasquan to California was gruelling, and the owner of the *Casco*, Dr Merritt, proved less eager to lease his property than the Stevensons were to get on board. Several weeks went by before a bargain was struck, and even then Dr Merritt was so horrified by Louis's gaunt physique that he privately ordered the ship's master, Captain Otis, to take everything he would require for a burial at sea. Fanny and Maggie, on the advice of Belle Strong, bought *holakus*, the loose, waistless gowns introduced to the South Seas by missionaries averse to the display of human flesh; Fanny loved them and would wear them until the end of her life, but Maggie missed her corsets and was probably aware of the incongruity of a *holaku* and a starched white widow's cap. Fanny bought provisions, salt pork, tinned food, champagne and copious supplies of tobacco, while Louis, on Lloyd's behalf, invested in an expensive camera and typewriter. It was 28 June before the *Casco*, carrying Louis, Maggie, Fanny, Lloyd and Valentine, and crewed by Captain Otis, four hands and a cook, was ready to be towed beyond the Golden Gate into the open sea.

For Louis, the last year had been one of leave-taking, of casting off, one by one, the places and the people he had known. As the *Casco's* sails filled and the western landfall of America fell back into the mist, yet another chapter of his life quietly came to a close.

CHAPTER 15

In the South Seas

I would like to rise and go
Where the golden apples grow;
Where below another sky
Parrot islands anchored lie.

– 'Travel', *A Child's Garden of Verses*, 1885 –

FOR THE NEXT two years, the Stevensons sailed the Pacific, visiting the
Marquesas, the Paumotu (now called Tuamoto) archipelago, Tahiti, the
Sandwich Islands and Hawaii. They experienced the horrors of Pacific
storms, received hospitality from islanders not long weaned, as Maggie
noted, from cannibalism, feasted on tropical food, and heard the wind
rustling in palm branches along stainless sands. Louis later wrote in *The
Wrecker* that 'day after day, the air had the same indescribable liveliness
and sweetness, soft and nimble, and as cool on the cheek as health. Day
after day, the sun flamed; night after night the moon beaconed or the
stars paraded their lustrous regiment.' Louis still caught colds, but only
in Fakarava in the Paumotus was he seriously ill, causing the *Casco* to
make a run for Papeete, the capital of Tahiti.

Here Louis encountered a new face of the islands. Tahiti was a
French colony, and Papeete full of colonial administrators and with a
population of Tahitians, Chinese, mixed-race and misfits from Europe.
The town was squalid and Louis hated it, later describing it as 'hell' in
his novel *The Ebb-tide*. He was fortunate, however, to be taken under
the wing of a Tahitian noblewoman, Princess Moë, and a local chief, Ori
a Ori, who lent the Stevensons a house in the village of Tautira on the
quieter side of the island. As he recovered, Louis wrote ballads based on
Polynesian legends, 'The Feast of Famine' and 'The Song of Rahero', and
worked on the closing chapters of *The Master of Ballantrae*, interrupted
earlier by the ructions over 'The Nixie'. He was already planning a book

about his island adventures, and a translation of poems and traditional tales of Tahiti. He took to wearing a *pareu*, a cotton sarong, and putting a flower behind his ear – a development gleefully reported by Fanny to his friends in England.

Delayed by the need to repair the main mast of the *Casco*, the Stevensons did not leave Tahiti until Christmas Day, 1888. It took a month to reach Hawaii, where the *Casco's* voyage was to end. In the capital, Honolulu, the voyagers were joined by Belle and Joe Strong and their eight-year-old son Austin, who had been living among the islands since 1882. It seems likely that Belle, impressed in San Francisco by the wealth lavished on fitting out the *Casco*, had decided to modify her hostility to her stepfather; Louis now assumed responsibility for this sullen, extravagant young woman and her alcoholic husband and child. After the *Casco* had sailed for San Francisco, the whole family – minus Valentine Roch, who had had one row too many with Fanny and departed to California in the huff – settled down for five months in Waikiki. Here Louis met Kalakaua, the last of the Hawaiian kings, and felt the first stirring of interest in the politics of Polynesia. Seeing how the region was losing its cultural identity and language when faced with the incursion of western colonial power, he began to draw parallels with the situation of the Scottish Highlanders after the 1745 Jacobite Rebellion when, in his view, Gaelic culture was brutally suppressed by an alien force.

In June 1889, overcoming his lifelong horror of ugliness and contagion for the sake of experience, Louis paid a visit to the leper settlement on the offshore island of Molokai, where the feared rejects of society were segregated in the care of a Roman Catholic mission. Until two months earlier, the director had been Father Damien (Joseph Veuster, 1840-89), a Belgian priest whose hands-on care for the diseased and dying ended with his own death from the same affliction. Louis was deeply affected by the suffering he saw on Molokai, the stoicism of the lepers and the dedication of the missionaries who toiled to alleviate it. A lapsed Presbyterian with the built-in antipathy to Catholic doctrine typical of his time and sect, he could still admire disinterested heroism. When, eight months after his visit, he read a vitriolic denunciation of Father Damien's alleged coarseness and immorality by a Presbyterian minister of Honolulu, the Rev. Dr C. M. Hyde, he wrote in the white heat of indignation a magnificent defence of the priest and his work on Molokai. As much a diatribe against the 'unco guid' faction he so disliked in Edinburgh as a personal attack, 'Father Damien: An Open

Letter to the Reverend Dr Hyde of Honolulu' was first published in the *Australian Star* newspaper in May 1890. Louis expected, with some justification, to be sued for libel, but Dr Hyde wisely decided to let the matter rest.

In May 1889 Maggie Stevenson had returned to Edinburgh to be with her sister, whom she wrongly thought to be dying. Louis said that he would follow her. He even toyed with the idea of settling in Madeira to be within easier reach of London, but the truth was that by this time the reasons for returning to Europe were fading. He wrote wistfully to Sidney Colvin:

> I feel as if I were untrue to friendship; believe me, Colvin, when I look forward to this absence for another year, my conscience sinks … but I think you will pardon me if you consider how much this tropical weather mends my health. … It seems it would be madness to come home now, with an imperfect book, no illustrations to speak of, and perhaps fall sick again by autumn.

All of which is true, but Louis also felt that friendship had failed him; although he and Henley had exchanged conciliatory letters and Henley, who had become the father of a little girl in 1888, was accepting articles and poems from Louis for the *Scots Observer* which he was currently editing, their former closeness was irrecoverable. There were, Louis admitted to Henry James, 'only seven or eight people in England, and one or two in the States' whom he would be sorry not to see again.

Before making up his mind finally, Louis, partly for his health and partly to collect more material for his projected book on the South Seas, decided to take another cruise. He was able to book accommodation on a new schooner, the *Equator*, which would trade in copra (coconut kernels) among the islands before berthing in Sydney, Australia. Joe Strong was to be taken along to paint lantern slides for Lloyd, whose latest money-making wheeze was to give illustrated lectures about their travels, but Belle's assumption that she and Austin would also be enjoying an expenses-paid holiday proved a false one. Egged on by Fanny, whose relationship with her daughter had always been prickly, Louis informed Belle that she and Austin would travel straight to Sydney where they would have to manage on a small allowance until the cruising party caught up with them. This did not go down well, and Belle's relationship with Louis again hit rock bottom.

The *Equator* left Honolulu in June for a six-month voyage, heading south through the Gilbert Islands to Samoa. At Apemama in the Gilberts, the Stevenson party left the ship for two months, receiving hospitality from King Tembinok, an enormously fat and volatile polygamist who ruled his three-island kingdom with a shotgun. The Stevensons, however, found favour; quaint houses on stilts were provided, and Fanny was invited to help herself to furnishings from the enormous storehouse where Tembinok kept his vast collection of European goods – everything from mirrors and French clocks to surgical instruments and garden tools. Servants were provided to look after the visitors, and Louis was even cured of a cold by the incantations of native magicians. King Tembinok wept to see the Stevensons rejoin the *Equator*, unaware that he would be immortalised in a lively account first published in the New York *Sun* and, with other essays, in the book *In the South Seas* in 1891.

On 7 December the *Equator* reached Apia, the port and main town of Upolu, a steep forested island in the Samoan archipelago. The ship was turning about quickly for the run to Australia, so it left without the Stevensons who wanted to stay awhile. On the day of their arrival, a London missionary, the Rev. W. E. Clarke, received an unforgettable impression of the family in the main street of Apia. Fanny, he recalled, was wearing a print gown, large gold ear-rings, a straw hat adorned with shells, and had a guitar slung across her back. Lloyd was wearing striped pyjamas, a straw hat and dark blue glasses, and was carrying a banjo. Louis, meanwhile, was dressed in tatty white flannels and a peaked yachting cap, had a cigarette in his mouth and a camera in his hand. Both men were barefoot and Mr Clarke assumed that this was a party of wandering minstrels, forced by hardship to travel cheaply in a trading ship.

It is hard to see how such a family could ever have fitted into prim English society again, and Louis probably sensed that too. During the two months that he spent on Upolu, he stayed with a wealthy American trader, Harry J. Moors, while Fanny and Lloyd were put up at a cottage inland. Moors took the family on a tour of the island, and urged an already half-willing Louis to buy a vacant estate at Vailima, 'the place of five waters' on the cool slope of the island's towering Mount Vaea. Initially Louis had some reservations; he disliked the dominant German influence on Samoa, and found the Samoans courteous but not entirely honest. Samoa, he admitted to Charles Baxter, was not as beautiful as the Marquesas or Tahiti, with 'a tamer face of nature' due to the acreage

of German-owned palm plantations, and he disliked the waterfront of
Apia, which vied with Papeete for corruption and squalor. But he praised
the waterfalls and rivers, which reminded him of the modest waters of
the Lothians and, although he had no illusions about the difficulty of
making money from a plantation, he liked the idea of being a 'laird' with
his own estate. Nor did Samoa seem totally remote; ships sailed regu-
larly to Australia and the United States, and mail to Europe was, for those
days, fast and reliable. Before he left for Sydney, Louis had bought 314 1/2
acres of Upolu, containing woods, rivers, cliffs and much undeveloped
scrubland. He consoled himself for the cost with thoughts of self-suffi-
ciency for himself and the idle clan he supported.

It was during this first stay in Samoa that Louis wrote a story based
on a German legend he had heard in Hawaii. 'The Bottle Imp' concerns
a Faustian pact between a demon and the owner of the bottle, who could
have any wish granted provided he promised the demon his immortal
soul. The only way to break this dangerous arrangement was for the
owner of the bottle to sell it for less than he paid for it. The story was
published in the *New York Herald* in 1891, but had an unexpected impact in Samoa when it was translated by a missionary and published in
the native language. The literally-minded Samoans, already wondering
how a down-at-heel storyteller like Stevenson could be rich enough to
buy Vailima, immediately thought they had the answer. His assumed
ownership of the imp in a bottle gave Louis a magician's status and the
honorific title 'Tusitala', the Teller of Tales.

* * *

Louis gave Moors instructions to have part of the estate cleared and a
cottage erected as a temporary home while the main house was being
built. Meanwhile Fanny and Louis, who had not seen a great deal of
each other during their Samoan stay, sailed for Sydney on the German-
owned SS *Lübeck*, Lloyd and Joe Strong having gone on ahead. Their
intention was to meet up with Belle and Austin Strong, then continue to
England to sell Skerryvore and wind up their affairs. The ship was clean
and efficiently run and the weather fine, so it should have been a pleasant
voyage. Louis, however, spent it worrying about the future of the
Strongs; Joe had failed to paint the lantern slides as agreed, ruining
Lloyd's big idea, and he was so often drunk that the chance of his ever
working at all was remote. Louis liked Joe personally and was reluctant

to abandon him, but that he was an undeserved burden could not be denied. He also shrank from the task of informing his friends that he intended to leave Europe for good, although he reflected bitterly that with Bob, Katharine and Henley estranged, Colvin and Baxter were the only friends he had left there.

Whatever his plans for telling them face to face, however, they were never fulfilled; after only a few weeks in Sydney, just as he was beginning to meet local artists and writers and enjoy exploring a new city, Louis was struck down by a heavy cold and had to take to his bed. All the old Bournemouth symptoms developed: high temperature, sore throat, violent coughing, pleurisy and finally haemorrhage. Desperate to get Louis to sea again, but prevented by a seamen's strike from getting the kind of berths she wanted, Fanny was obliged to approach the captain of the SS *Janet Nicholl*, a small trading ship bound for the Gilbert Islands with a crew of kanakas, indentured labourers from the Pacific islands who were not affected by the strike. Not unnaturally, the captain was leery about taking a dying man on board, but Fanny on the warpath was a force beyond nature. On 11 April Louis was carried on board on a stretcher, once again with Lloyd in tow.

As usual Louis recovered at sea, and before returning to Vailima in July had visited New Zealand, the Ellis Islands, the Marshall Islands and New Caledonia. While the *Janet Nicholl* traded in the Gilbert Islands, he took the opportunity to visit King Tembinok in Apemama, but found him in a sour mood due to an epidemic of measles then ravaging his kingdom – like so many diseases, an unwanted gift from the white man.

Fanny said later that the extended voyage on the *Janet Nicholl* was the happiest time of her life. There has been speculation in recent biographies about the marital relations of the Stevensons, which must have been affected both by Louis's violent illnesses and Fanny's hypochondria and depressions. So it is interesting to know that on this voyage Fanny thought she was pregnant, and later told Will Low that she had miscarried. Since she was now 50 this seems unlikely, so presumably Louis was not as upset as when a similar incident occurred in 1883. Then he had written to Walter Simpson that, although he thought he had never wanted children, 'When the alarm passed off – I was inconsolable!' Although he shrank from the sight of children suffering, and shared the pain and desolation of friends when a child died, he loved the company of children and clearly was sometimes saddened by the lack of his own. This is the only valid explanation for his blindness to the faults of his stepson Lloyd Osbourne, and his insistence that the work-shy, un-talented youth was a worthy collaborator. Lloyd would boast later that the best chapters of *The Wrecker* were his, and the swank and self-aggrandisement evident in his *An Intimate Portrait of R.L.S.* (1924) is quite repellent. Yet as Stevenson's most recent biographer, Claire Harman, perceptively remarks, 'In truth, it was hardly [Lloyd's] fault if he got the impression that his contribution to the works of RLS were invaluable, and that he was a true heir, not just to his stepfather's semi-miraculous money-making capacity, but to the genius.'

*   *   *

Louis and Fanny arrived back in Apia in September 1890 to find that Moors had cleared a dozen acres and put up a house, a two-storeyed, tin-roofed cottage with family accommodation upstairs and space below for the head workman, his wife and child, and three kanakas. The kitchen was a separate building eight yards distant, a problem in the rainy season, as Fanny immediately complained; indeed, she complained about every-thing from the colour of the interior walls to the lack of pigpens and chicken-runs. There was no furniture other than beds they had brought from Sydney, and there would be none until Lloyd, who had gone to England to sell Skerryvore and escort Maggie Stevenson back to Vailima, had arranged the shipment to Samoa of their goods and chattels. The roof leaked and when there was a storm the rain drummed deafeningly and the lamps blew out in the wind. Louis, who had hated storms ever since he was a child in Edinburgh, and once told Colvin that 'in my hell, it would always blow a gale', shuddered as the tempests screamed over the island and whipped wildly through the trees.

Fanny, in conditions reminiscent of Silverado, set to work to make a kitchen garden in the clearing. She was helped by a Samoan factotum named Henry Simile, whom Louis initially disliked but came to value, particularly since Simile proved a tactful go-between in the mutual hostilities of Fanny and the outdoor workforce. When she was not bawling at the kanakas, Fanny did what she did best, planting seeds of melon, pineapple, bean, tomato and mango, while Louis, who had never felt better, helped enthusiastically with the weeding. In the upstairs sitting-room of the cottage, he finished his South Seas letters, put the finishing touches to *The Wrecker*, and sketched the outline of a new novel, *The Ebb-tide*.

Louis also plucked up the courage to write the letters he had been dreading, finally informing Sidney Colvin, Fanny Sitwell, Charles Baxter and Henry James that they would look in vain for his return. That he felt some bitterness about their lack of comprehension of his true reasons is clear from a letter to Fanny Sitwell:

> I beg you all to remember that, though I take my sicknesses with a decent face, they do represent suffering, and weakness, and painful disability; as well as the loss of all that makes animal life desirable.

The disquiet expressed by Colvin is, however, understandable; he had been Louis's supporter and loyal agent since they first met at Cockfield Rectory 17 years before, and he genuinely believed that Louis's preoccupation with the South Seas would ruin his literary reputation. His personal disappointment is also a tribute to the fun of Louis's company, now lost to his friends unless they were willing to make the long, arduous journey to Samoa.

Meanwhile, the Samoan forest, with its rank luxuriance and primeval silence broken only by wild, sudden bird and animal cries, was impacting on Louis's imagination. In the 'Woodman' he wrote:

> *Thick round me in the teeming mud*
> *Briar and fern strove to the blood:*
> *The hooked liana in her gin*
> *Noosed his reluctant neighbours in:*
> *There the green murderer strove and spread,*
> *Upon his smothering victims fed.*

One day as they worked in the 'teeming mud' of the clearing in the forest, Louis and Fanny had unexpected visitors, who inevitably turned up just when the Stevensons were coal-black and sweating in an attempt to set up a greasy cooking stove. These were an American painter John La Farge, and his friend Henry Brooks Adams, a Harvard professor of history and the descendant of two American presidents. Adams, who liked neither the British nor Americans whom he considered of a lower class than his own, was predisposed to sneer at the Stevensons, but his snide description still rings true. Louis, he said, was a man 'so thin and emaciated that he looked like a bundle of sticks in a bag, with dirty striped pyjamas, the baggy legs tucked into coarse woollen stockings, one of which was bright brown in colour, the other a purplish dark tone'. Fanny was 'in the usual missionary nightgown which was no cleaner than her husband's shirt and drawers, but she omitted the stockings. Her complexion and eyes were dark and strong, like a half-breed Mexican.' As for the house, it was 'a two-story Irish shanty' and 'squalid as a railway navvy's board hut'. This last impression, at least, was shared by Maggie Stevenson, who arrived, shuddered, and left immediately to spend two months with cousins in the Antipodes. Fortunately, in another part of the clearing, a very different house was arising from the mud.

CHAPTER 16

A Laird in Samoa

Blows the wind today, and the sun and the rain are flying,
Blows the wind on the moors today and now,
Where about the graves of the martyrs the whaups are crying,
My heart remembers how!

Grey recumbent tombs of the dead in desert places,
Standing-stones on the vacant wine-red moor,
Hills of sheep, and the howes of the silent vanished races,
And winds, austere and pure.

Be it granted to me to behold you again in dying,
Hills of home! And to hear again the call,
Hear above the graves of the martyrs the peewees crying,
And hear no more at all.

– 'To S. R. Crockett, On receiving a Dedication', 1893

IN JANUARY 1891 Louis had gone alone to Sydney to meet his mother and Lloyd on their return from the United Kingdom. 'Old Mrs Stevenson', aged 61, had decided to burn her boats in Edinburgh and move permanently to Samoa; 17 Heriot Row was to be let and the most precious furnishings shipped to Vailima. Her disappointment at the squalid conditions in the temporary cottage must have been severe. Once more the climate of Sydney had played havoc with Louis's lungs, forcing a longer absence than he intended, and reinforcing his belief that he could only ever be healthy in the South Seas. In April the new house was ready and the family moved in.

Vailima was handsome; a spacious, two-storeyed mansion with peacock blue walls and a red tin roof, it had shutters to keep out the gales and a verandah running, at both levels, along its north-facing side. The dining-room was papered with yellow *tapa* and curtained in yellow and silver silk, and on the ground floor was a vast hall, panelled and with a ceiling of Californian redwood. Water was piped to the kitchen and bathroom from storage tanks behind the house; and as well as bedrooms and a library, there was a study for Louis with a writing-table, book-shelves and a narrow camp-style bed. When the furniture from 17 Heriot Row and Skerryvore arrived, the house acquired mahogany and rose-wood tables and chairs, a Chippendale sideboard, silver, wine glasses, mirrors, a grand piano, a sculpture by Rodin, paintings and books.

In 1892 another two-storey block was added, and the temporary house, now named 'Pineapple Cottage', improved, in the first instance for the Strongs. Bowing to the inevitable, Louis had invited Belle, Joe and Austin to join the Vailima household, which was famously photo-graphed in May 1892 by the local postmaster John Davis. Later, when the drunken and opium-addicted Joe had finally been sent packing, the cottage became a bachelor residence for Lloyd. The great hall of Vailima, through Louis's fame and the opulence of the Stevensons' entertaining, soon became an exotic social centre. Louis and Fanny hosted dinners and even balls, and Samoan chiefs rubbed shoulders with European dignitaries of several nations. On these occasions, Fanny changed her *holaku* for an elegant silk gown, and Louis, who had always enjoyed dressing up, appeared resplendent in a white mess jacket and silk shirt. The Samoan servants, in what appeared to some observers as a whim-sical conceit, but which had a symbolic significance for Louis, were dressed in sarongs of Royal Stewart tartan. As he passed his 40th birth-day there was a notable change in Louis; he appears for the first time, both in photographs and in the magnificent portrait by Girolamo Pieri Nerli in 1893, as a man, rather than as a boy with long hair and a moustache.

Louis was free of illness at this period of his life, but not free of anxiety. He had borrowed a large sum of money from Harry J. Moors to pay for the building of the house, to be repaid from future earnings which, in view of his poor health, he reckoned an unreliable source of in-come. Maggie, generous but never thrifty, was insatiable in her demands for the grandeur she felt Louis's fame deserved; Fanny and Belle were casually extravagant, and Lloyd a lazy fellow, always in need of expen-sive holidays and with ideas above his station. A glance at the photo-graph of family and servants on the verandah shows all too clearly the number of dependants Louis had to feed and house. Although officially

Belle and Lloyd were supposed to have jobs, Belle as housekeeper and Lloyd as estate manager, their performances in these roles were derisory, while Joe was a lost cause. Only Fanny, as head gardener, really pulled her weight, but her poor relationship with the outdoor servants created another problem.

A parallel has often been drawn between Sir Walter Scott's building of Abbotsford, his dream house in the Scottish Borders, and the building of Vailima (indeed, Louis himself once referred to Vailima as 'sub-Priorsford'), but it was not only overworking to pay for an extravagant lifestyle that the two greatest Scottish novelists had in common. Both had a romantic idea of pre-1745 Highland society in which the clan, with its family members and retainers, owed honour and loyalty to the munificent chief; the lavish hospitality and the tartan sarongs were a manifestation of this ideal. This model of a closely-knit, interdependent society may also be the clue to the 'Vailima Prayers', written to be read at a daily gathering of family and servants and posthumously published, to the puzzlement of those who knew that Louis had long since abandoned belief in God. Fanny, in a cloying preface, claimed that the Samoan servants expected this ritual, but it is unlikely that anyone except for Maggie really cared about it. Childless and an only child, Louis's life at Vailima was the price he had to pay, not for the family he wanted, but for the family he had got.

*　*　*

Although he was often working in his study for ten hours a day, Louis found time to involve himself in Samoan politics, sometimes to an extent unwise in a foreign national. In the 1880s Germany, Britain and the United States (the 'Great Powers') all had an interest in the Islands which, besides their trading potential, provided a useful refuelling station for coal-fired shipping. After a conference in Berlin in 1889, tripartite control of the Samoan government was established; the claim to kingship of Chief Laupepa was officially recognised, while the (equally valid) claim of Chief Mataafa was rejected. Louis, who had begun to learn the Samoan language and had a sophisticated understanding of the complex structure of Samoan society, saw his self-appointed role as a conciliator, at the same time as champion of Mataafa, of whom he was fond. He sent long letters to *The Times* in London, drawing attention to the inadequacies of the German administrators, and in 1892 wrote *A Footnote to*

History, a highly critical account of German involvement in Samoan affairs and the role of the British and Americans in the 'settlement' that followed.

Just as he had risked a libel suit over his defence of Father Damien, Louis now risked a fine, imprisonment or even deportation for this airing of anti-establishment views, and was really only saved by the embarrassment his arrest would have caused to the Colonial Office in London. When, in 1893, war erupted between Laupepa and Mataafa – a war which came uncomfortably close to Vailima – Laupepa won easily with the support of the colonial powers who had instated him. Mataafa was deported, with the more important among his supporters, to the Marshall Islands. Louis wrote and sent gifts to Mataafa, and tried unsuccessfully to secure Mataafa's pardon; he also visited and gave aid to the lesser chiefs imprisoned in Apia who, on their release, rewarded his loyalty by building a road to connect Vailima to the main Apia thoroughfare. This 'Road of the Loving Heart' was a touching and fitting tribute to a man who had followed his conscience and risked the consequences; Louis responded in his usual warm fashion by organising a vast celebratory feast in the great hall at Vailima.

*　　*　　*

It would be pleasant to think that in the last years of his life, Louis's reputation made, his vigour restored and his household established, he was finally happy. Sadly this was not so, since he had other problems besides money. Lloyd had taken a young Samoan woman as his mistress but refused to marry her, enraging his stepfather who, despite having his own youthful affairs flung in his face by his adopted son, insisted that when a young man had seduced a respectable woman, honour required an offer of marriage. Fanny settled matters by giving the unfortunate girl her marching orders, but the behaviour of Lloyd cast a long shadow over a relationship which Louis had so stubbornly believed to be perfect.

Worse was to come. Since their arrival at Vailima in 1890, Fanny had been struggling with depression. Early on, a light-hearted remark made by Louis that she had 'the soul of a peasant' made her feel that her contribution to the marriage was undervalued; she brooded and became ever more suspicious of slights. However much Fanny enjoyed dressing up and acting as a great writer's consort, she was dissatisfied with her life; her own writing ambition was largely unrealised, and she felt that her criticism of Louis's work was increasingly ignored. The relationship of Fanny and Louis was described by Fanny's biographer Margaret Mackay as 'a passionate friendship', but by this time it seems that even the friendship was beginning to cool.

Fanny and Louis now slept apart, he in his study and she in her redwood-panelled bedroom upstairs. Whether or not Fanny really had become pregnant on board the *Janet Nicholl*, her failure to have a child with Louis probably hurt more because she knew it was now too late and, if she was brooding about babies, dark memories of Hervey would naturally have surfaced in her mind. She certainly resented Louis's growing intimacy with Belle who, after Joe's departure and the sending of Austin to be educated with Louis Sanchez in Monterey, had wisely buried the hatchet with her stepfather. When Louis began to suffer from writer's cramp, Belle offered to be his amanuensis; this meant that they spent much time together in Louis's study, excluding Fanny. Louis's unguarded description of his wife, written in April 1893 to his fellow novelist and admirer J. M. Barrie, paints an alarming picture: '... a violent enemy, a brimstone friend; is always either loathed or slavishly adored; indifference impossible. The natives think her uncanny and that devils serve her. Dreams dreams and sees visions.' A few months later this damaged woman, who had teetered so often on the verge of breakdown, collapsed completely, suffering hallucinations and periods of hysteria so violent that Louis and Belle had to take turns to sleep in her room. Louis, mindful of her care of him when he was ill, was gentle and attentive, but a holiday in Sydney, which he hoped would do her good, in fact only did him harm. Fanny's recovery was slow, and Louis watched over her with mixed feelings of hope and terror of relapse.

* * *

In the midst of all this domestic turbulence, Louis went on writing. It was what he lived for and, as his youth receded, his insight deepened and experience widened the scope of his work. His years in the Pacific had given him a new world to explore but, for all his immersion in Samoan culture and politics, his South Seas fiction is far from starry-eyed. 'The Beach of Falesá' tells of a white trader named Wiltshire who takes a native wife and falls foul of an evil rival, Case, who invokes native taboos to achieve his ends. It is notable for its realistic depiction of 'beach' life, and for being the work in which Louis at last managed to write openly about a sexual relationship. But its 'happy ending' is qualified. Looking on his mixed-race daughters, Wiltshire speaks bleakly of the fate of such children a century ago: 'I can't reconcile myself to their taking up with Kanakas, and I'd like to know where I'm to find the whites?'

The Ebb-tide, a novel supposedly but not actually written in collaboration with Lloyd, holds not even a hint of optimism. It is a chilling study of three flawed and amoral beachcombers, Herrick, Davis and Huish, who steal a ship abandoned after an outbreak of smallpox, but loaded, as they believe, with a cargo of champagne, most of which turns out to be water. Losing their bearings and landing on a remote island, they fall into the clutches of Attwater, its ruthless, fanatical white ruler, who plays on their weaknesses, thwarts their ambitions and, in different ways, destroys them. As much as *Strange Case of Dr Jekyll and Mr Hyde*, *The Ebb-tide* probes personal conflict and the nature of evil; Louis himself called it 'as grim a tale as ever was written, and as grimy, and as hateful', and its conclusion is deeply depressing.

For all that he had absorbed himself so eagerly in Samoan affairs, towards the end of his life Louis experienced a strong sense of exile, and memories of his homeland – fed by screeds of material sent by Andrew Lang for a historical trilogy which Louis planned but never wrote – flooded his mind. He conjured up the lost landscape of his youth, yet it was not the Scotland of the 1860s, about which he wrote so beautifully in 'The Coast of Fife' and 'The Education of an Engineer', that he longed for, far less the industrialised Scotland of the late nineteenth century. Rather the Scotland for which Louis felt nostalgic was a country of the imagination, one gone for over a century before he was born, the Scotland of honour and loyalty to chieftain and family, which he had tried to recreate at Vailima with such indifferent success.

His first foray from Samoa into this territory was in his novel *Catriona*, the long-awaited sequel to *Kidnapped*, which continued the adventures of David Balfour. *Kidnapped* was a hard act to follow, and *Catriona*, which centres on a dissection of the Appin murder trial, never achieved the same popularity. This is partly because of the stolidity of the mature David Balfour, and partly because the vital presence of Alan Breck Stewart is missing throughout most of the narrative; it is also noticeable that, despite having written 'The Beach at Falesá', Louis's attempt to portray a credible love relationship in a Scottish novel failed. But the use of the Scots language and the evocation of the land, from Argyllshire to the East Lothian coast and the environs of Edinburgh, are magnificent, while the supernatural short story embedded in the narrative, 'The Tale of Tod Lapraik', another exploration of the divided personality, bears comparison with 'Wandering Willie's Tale' in Scott's *Redgauntlet*. It also has a worthy successor in 'The Legend of the Black Jaws' from *The Testament of Gideon Mack* by the contemporary Scottish novelist James Robertson.

At the beginning of 1894 Louis had two uncompleted novels in his files. *St Ives*, which relates the adventures of a French prisoner-of-war after his escape from Edinburgh Castle during the Napoleonic wars, was set partly in Edinburgh and Swanston Cottage, scenes of Louis's youthful days, and partly in England. Often unfairly dismissed as a potboiler, *St Ives* has a pacey, vibrant narrative and memorable characters. Left unfinished at Louis's death, it was thought worth completing in two versions: the first, at Colvin's behest, by Sir Arthur Quiller-Couch in 1897, the second in 1990 by the Stevenson scholar Jenni Calder. *Weir of Hermiston*, of which Louis had written a few chapters in 1892 under the title of *The Justice-Clerk,* is a work of a different stamp. It is a dark tale of conflict between a father, Lord Weir, modelled on the notoriously brutal eighteenth-century Scottish judge Lord Braxfield, and his fastidious son Archie. Played out in the streets of Edinburgh and in the bleak, glowering landscape of the Scottish borderland, the story has the tragic inevitability of the Border ballads, echoes of the Old Testament, and all the subtle character-analysis – this time of women as well as men – of a novelist coming to the peak of his powers. Even incomplete, it has a claim to be considered as Louis's finest achievement.

In the autumn of 1894 Louis himself sank into depression. The heat was overpowering, and he was suffering from a sore throat, severe indigestion and swelling of his legs. His underlying problems were not, however, only physical; he had been powerfully affected by Fanny's collapse and his quarrel with Lloyd. He was beset by money worries and feelings of guilt about his father and, most fearfully of all, he suspected that his creativity was fading. The thought of an early death, which had so infuriated him as a 17-year-old in the carpenter's house in Anstruther, had ceased to trouble him; to his oldest friend, Charles Baxter, he wrote: 'I have been so long waiting for death, I have unwrapped my thoughts from about life so long, that I have not a filament left to hold by; I have done my fiddling so long under Vesuvius that I have almost forgotten to play, and can only wait for the eruption, and I think it long of coming.' Of his constant dreaming of the land of his childhood, his biographer

Frank McLynn remarks that 'those psychoanalysts who believe in the "death drive" would regard this as a sign of the unconscious preparing ignorantly for its extinction' – a theory that has received support from recent research studies in the biology of the brain.

Baxter, believing from his management of Louis's affairs that the root cause of his state of mind was financial, was in touch with Sidney Colvin, and together they devised a plan for a limited 'Edinburgh Edition' of Louis's collected works. This idea pleased Louis, who set to work to write prefaces, although few of these were ever completed. He also took up *Weir of Hermiston* and found his old enthusiasm returning as he once more trod the heather hills and heard the old Scots language in his mind. He wrote a poem which he tucked into the manuscript, intending it to form a dedication to Fanny, perhaps a last plea for her understanding of a passion he knew she had never been able to share:

> *I saw rain falling and the rainbow drawn*
> *On Lammermuir. Hearkening I heard again*
> *In my precipitous city beaten bells*
> *Winnow the keen sea wind. And here afar,*
> *Intent on my own race and place, I wrote. ...*

Like the famous poem he wrote to thank his fellow writer S. R. Crockett for the dedication of his novel *The Stickit Minister*, these lines are the pure essence of Robert Louis Stevenson's love for his native land, the country he crossed the world to avoid, but could never really leave.

* * *

On Tuesday 13 November 1894, Louis's 44th birthday was celebrated at Vailima with customary pomp and extravagance. A whole heifer was roasted, along with pigs and chickens; there were also yams, bananas, pineapples and arrowroot puddings. Ever an optimist, Maggie wrote in her diary how thankful she was that her son had 'been spared to see his 44th birthday in so much health and comfort'. Less than three weeks later, on Monday 3 December, Louis was up early, ready to work on the ninth chapter of *Weir of Hermiston* with Belle; he felt that the book was coming along well and was eager to push ahead. His most pressing problem that morning was Fanny, who had always believed she was psychic and for the last couple of days had been oppressed by the feeling that something dreadful was going to happen. Louis, knowing his wife's fragile mental state, pointed out that the Vailima family was safe at home; the only person they knew on the high seas was his cousin Graham Balfour, a frequent visitor to Vailima who had gone to visit Mataafa in the Marshall Islands. Mid-morning he took a break and tried to amuse Fanny with a card game and a reading of his latest chapter, then he went back to work. In the afternoon he dictated letters, rode to Apia and back, and went for a swim.

Coming downstairs after changing into fresh clothes, Louis found Fanny still swathed in gloom. Suggesting that they should make a dish of what they called 'Vailima salad', he went down to the cellar to bring up a bottle of wine. He was on the verandah mixing lime juice and oil to make a mayonnaise, and chatting animatedly to Fanny when suddenly he stopped and put both hands to his head. 'Oh, what a pain!' he cried. 'Do I look strange?' Fanny barely had time to say 'No', before he collapsed onto his knees.

With the help of the Samoan butler, Fanny lifted Louis and half-carried him to his grandfather's chair in the great hall; by then he had lost consciousness. Fanny held brandy to his lips, screaming for Maggie, who came running, while Belle rushed to fetch Lloyd from Pineapple Cottage. Louis was still open-eyed and breathing heavily, so while Fanny rubbed more brandy into his wrists and tried to rouse him, Lloyd mounted a horse and raced down to Apia to fetch a doctor. Two came, the local physician Dr Funk and Dr Anderson the surgeon on HMS *Wallaroo*, then at anchor in Apia harbour. They agreed that Louis had suffered a cerebral haemorrhage, and told Fanny sadly that nothing could be done. Louis died without regaining consciousness at 8.10 pm.

There was no great clamour in the house. Numb with shock, Fanny and Maggie laid out the corpse in dress trousers and a white shirt, and two of the young servants put Louis's hands together in an attitude of prayer. The news spread like wildfire, and all through the evening the local chiefs and their families came to pay their respects. They covered the body with finely woven mats and quietly said their farewells. '*Tofa, Tusitala,*' they murmured. '*Alofa, Tusitala.*'

* * *

In the tropics, decomposition of a body is swift, and the doctors said that Louis must be buried by three o'clock the next day. He had wanted to be buried on the summit of Mount Vaea, high above the forest and the ocean; the problem was that there was no road from Vailima to the mountain top. Determined to fulfil Louis's wish, Fanny called for the help of the chiefs who had built the 'Road of the Loving Heart', and they did not let her or Louis down. This was another labour of love; every capable individual came to help, and by midday on 4 December a path through the forest to the summit was hacked with machetes and axes. At one o'clock the Samoan pallbearers, carrying the coffin draped in the ensign from the *Casco* on their shoulders, began to toil up the slope. The Service for the Burial of the Dead was read, and the coffin lowered into a grave also prepared by Samoan friends. It was 1897 before the famous resting-place was completed, its cement blocks surmounted by a plinth bearing two bronze plaques. One tells in Samoan that this is 'the tomb of Tusitala'; the other carries the 'Requiem' that Louis had written on the train to Monterey 15 years before. After his short, impulsive, passionate life, he lay 'where he longed to be'.

Home is the sailor, home from sea,
And the hunter home from the hill.

CHAPTER 17

The Myth of
Robert Louis Stevenson

Had he lived another year, I should have seen him. All plans
arranged for a visit to Vailima, 'to settle on those shores for ever,'
he wrote, or something to that effect, 'and if my wife likes you what
a time you will have, and if she does not, how I shall pity you'.

– Sir J. M. Barrie, in *I Can Remember Robert Louis Stevenson*, 1922 –

IT TOOK SEVERAL weeks for the news of Louis's death to reach London,
bringing public grief and private consternation to his friends. Sidney
Colvin learned of it as he left a government office in Whitehall and
caught sight of a newspaper poster bearing the words, 'Death of R. L.
Stevenson'. Henry James came as close to hysteria as he ever did: 'It isn't
true, it isn't true, say it isn't *true*,' he wailed to Fanny Sitwell, who must
have had melancholy thoughts of her own. Most painfully situated of all
was Charles Baxter, who was already on his way to Samoa to deliver to
Louis in person the first two volumes of the 'Edinburgh Edition'. He
heard the news at Port Said, but decided to travel on to Vailima where,
two months later, Fanny received him with a coolness bordering on
discourtesy.

Maggie Stevenson had by then decided to head in the opposite
direction, unable to bear the painful memories that Vailima evoked.
Having only recently sold 17 Heriot Row, she returned to her sister's
house in Edinburgh, where her sad days were lightened by visits from
Louis's admirers. She was particularly gratified when called upon by
Lord Rosebery, who as Foreign Secretary in the early 1890s had supported Louis's hot-headed activities in Samoa against his more cautious
colleagues. But Maggie had nothing to live for, and died of pneumonia
in 1897. Her last words were: 'There is Louis! I must go.'

On Maggie's death, in accordance with her husband's will, the
whole of the Stevenson estate in Scotland passed to Fanny and Lloyd;

when added to what they had already inherited directly from Louis in property and literary rights, this bounty ensured that they would never be short of money again.

* * *

Elsewhere in Edinburgh another of the women in Louis's life was living with a sister and holding court among his acolytes. During the brief apotheosis of 'her laddie' in the first decade of the twentieth century, Alison Cunningham was much sought by readers of *A Child's Garden of Verses*, eager to sit at the feet of the angel who had inspired such devotion. Cummy was happy to reminisce and, despite her religious principles, equally happy to sell inscribed first editions of books by 'her laddie', and to distribute those most nineteenth-century of souvenirs – strands of his hair. She had taught him the grandeur of biblical language and the vocabulary and rhythm of the old Scots tongue, and he had attributed his dramatic sensibility to her. Yet it is hard not to wonder whether she ever realised that his whole life had been a rebellion against the hell-fire evangelicalism and Calvinist propaganda she had fed him in the nursery, or understood the themes of schism and duality that give his fiction such tension and power. She died after breaking her hip in a fall in 1910, aged 92.

Fanny stayed on at Vailima for a while, clinging to the hope that she could keep the estate running and with plans to diversify, possibly into the growing of ingredients for perfume. Realising finally that her ideas were impracticable, and that after Maggie's death it hardly mattered, she decided to live the rest of her life elsewhere. All of Vailima except the grave site was sold to a German merchant for £1750 – a paltry price compared with the lavish sum that had been spent creating it. When the Germans annexed Samoa in 1900, the house became the Governor's residence, a development that would surely have displeased Louis. After the First World War, Vailima was passed to the government of New Zealand, which then administered Samoa on behalf of the League of Nations. Then after Samoa achieved independence in 1962, it became the headquarters of the Samoan Head of State. Not until the 1990s did Vailima become a shrine to Stevenson's memory, the house beautifully restored by the Arizona-based Robert Louis Stevenson Museum/ Preservation Foundation.

*   *   *

Fanny intended to settle in the United States, but before that, accompanied by Lloyd, she travelled to Britain, intent on settling old scores. The first victim in her sights was Sidney Colvin, who had been asked by Louis to write his biography. However, this idea was displeasing to Fanny, partly because she did not like Colvin and partly because she was afraid that he knew too much. Fanny had known since the SS *Ludgate Hill* arrived in New York in 1887 that her husband was destined to become a legend in his own lifetime and, denied her own literary aspirations, had decided that the task of her widowhood was to preserve immaculate 'the myth of Robert Louis Stevenson', based on the icon of a saintly invalid nurtured and sustained by a loving and self-sacrificing wife. The idea of entrusting the biography to anyone who knew of Louis's youthful love life and the 'years of jink' was unthinkable; Colvin was, after all, friendly with Baxter and Henley, both of whom had beans to spill if they so chose. Fanny and Lloyd therefore arranged a meeting in London with Louis's cousin, Graham Balfour, who had spent long holidays at Vailima and was one of the few friends fortunate enough to be liked by Fanny. With minimal consultation of Colvin, they offered him the job.

Legally Fanny was within her rights. Louis's literary estate had been left to her, along with the right to be consulted about the biography, which he had seen primarily as a way of raising money for his heirs. And no one can blame Graham Balfour, an honourable man who would later be knighted for his years of service as a director of education, for jumping at the chance to write the life of a world-famous celebrity who happened to be his cousin. It is generally agreed too that, for a writer of no experience, he did a more than competent job. Two aspects of the business are, however, unpleasant: how Colvin, who had championed Louis's work long before he was famous, was bullied by the Osbournes into giving up a task which meant a great deal to him; and how Fanny contrived to control what did, and did not, go into *The Life of Robert Louis Stevenson* published in 1901. What she could not control was the critical reaction, polite on the whole, but in one instance very impolite indeed.

W. E. Henley had had little contact with Louis after 1890, when he received a black mark for failing to call on Maggie when he was working in Edinburgh and she was briefly back at 17 Heriot Row. In 1893, however, when the Henleys lost their much loved six-year-old daughter Margaret to meningitis, Louis was moved to write a warm letter of sympathy. Henley reciprocated with a letter which, Louis told Charles Baxter, was 'in very good taste and rather touching'. It was Fanny who, unable to think kindly of Henley even in such terrible circumstances, 'thought it was a letter preparatory to the asking of money'. Louis, deciding wrongly that it could be so construed, 'with a great deal of distaste' authorised Baxter to pay 'when necessary' five pounds a month to Henley. He then added, fatally: 'He can't starve at that; it's enough – more than he had when I first knew him, and if I gave him more it would only lead to his starting a gig and a Pomeranian dog.'

Even if allowances are made for Louis's anxiety about provision for Fanny and her children – he was also making grudging noises to Baxter about payments to Bob and Katharine – rarely can an act of generosity have sounded more ungracious and condescending. It is made no less so by the fact that Louis never imagined that the letter would be made public. So it was unfortunate that it came to the attention of Graham Balfour when he was writing the *Life*, more unfortunate still that Balfour quoted it, his only precaution being to replace Henley's name with the letter 'Z'. The 'Pomeranian dog' had been a silly joke between Louis and Henley in their youthful days, and as soon as Henley read the book he realised that the reference was to him. Invited to review *The Life of Robert Louis Stevenson* in the *Pall Mall Gazette*, this angry and wounded man went for the jugular in one of the most stunning pieces of invective ever to have appeared in print.

Beginning with his own distinction between 'the Stevenson who went to America in '87 and the Stevenson who never came back', Henley went on to complain that Balfour's portrayal of Stevenson as 'an angel clean from heaven' was not one he could recognise. He growled:

> Not if I can help it shall this faultless, or very nearly faultless, monster go down to after years as the Lewis [*sic*] I knew, and loved, and laboured with and for, with all my heart and understanding.

Declining to be concerned with 'this Seraph in Chocolate, this barley-sugar effigy of a real man' who was 'not my old, riotous, intrepid, scornful Stevenson at all', Henley proceeded to demolish the character and reputation of his former friend, detailing his personal vanity, his egotism, his political naiveté, and the condescension of a man who could

afford 'several kennels of Pomeranians and gigs innumerable'. Not even
Stevenson's courage in the face of illness was spared the lash:

> Are we not all stricken men? ... And why, because he wrote better
> than any one, should he be praised for what many a poor consump-
> tive seamstress does: cheerfully, faithfully, with no eloquent appeals
> to God, and not so much as a paragraph in the evening papers?

It is one of the most notorious flytings in literary history, energetic,
bitter, vengeful and tasteless, and sadly better known now than anything
else Henley ever wrote. Yet it is true that Graham Balfour's biography
was a far from candid account, and Henley was clearly gunning for the
censor. The review is as much an attack on Fanny Stevenson and her
attempts to manipulate the truth as on the friend who went to America
'and never came back'.

It is easy to forget that William Ernest Henley had a life, apart from
Robert Louis Stevenson. He enjoyed the company of young people and,
as editor of the *Scots Observer* (later the *National Observer*), showed
great talent in encouraging new writers; his contributors, collectively
nicknamed by Max Beerbohm 'the Henley Regatta', included the Irish
dramatist G. B. Shaw and poet W. B. Yeats, the Scots novelist and play-
wright J. M. Barrie, and Kenneth Grahame, author of *The Wind in the
Willows*. Henley's life was shattered by the death in 1893 of his daughter,
the little girl whom the poet Alice Meynell had called 'the Golden Child'
and who was Barrie's inspiration for Wendy in his play *Peter Pan*. In the
last years of his life he suffered chronic pain and increasing disability. He
died in 1903, aged 54.

*   *   *

Sidney Colvin's career as a professor and museum director in Cambridge
lasted until 1884, when he became keeper of the Department of Prints
and Drawings at the British Museum. Robbed of the opportunity to
write Stevenson's biography, he edited the 'Edinburgh Edition' of his
works, and produced an expurgated edition of his friend's letters which
is nowadays poorly regarded. His long intimacy with Mrs Fanny Sitwell
was finally formalised on 7 July 1903 at St Marylebone Parish Church,
where his friend Robert Browning had married Elizabeth Barrett more
than half a century before. This union of a 58-year-old bridegroom and

a 64-year-old bride, who had had to wait so long to be free, lasted happily for more than 20 years. Colvin was knighted in 1911, and both he and Lady Colvin made discreet contributions to *I Can Remember Robert Louis Stevenson* in 1922. Lady Colvin died in 1924, and Sir Sidney in 1927.

* * *

Once she had dealt with Sidney Colvin, Fanny turned her attention to Charles Baxter, the most faithful of Louis's friends, who had managed his business affairs with integrity and for little reward; he was also the driving force behind the 'Edinburgh Edition', which was paying considerable royalties into Fanny's coffers. Baxter himself had fallen on hard times, with a drink problem, a failing business and a family to support, but he got no help from Fanny. His stewardship was terminated and, although he lived until 1919, his connection with the Stevensons was over. Nor was Fanny more generous to Bob Stevenson, whom she had once loved; when Bob died in 1900, leaving a severely impoverished widow and two children, she went against Tom Stevenson's declared wishes and refused to offer assistance.

Although she would make two further visits to Europe, the latter part of Fanny's life was spent in the western United States, where she bought a Spanish-style house in Hyde Street, San Francisco, and a ranch at Ensenada in northern Mexico. For the final ten years she had a relationship with a man 40 years her junior. Edward (Ned) Salisbury Field, employed as a secretary, travelled everywhere with Fanny and was widely believed to be her lover. Fanny's house in San Francisco survived the earthquake and fire in 1906; firefighters, aware that it contained relics of Stevenson, gave it priority over other buildings. Fanny died there of a stroke in 1914, aged 74. Her ashes were taken back to Vailima and buried in Louis's tomb.

Although Fanny had left her personal estate, worth $589,000 (£120,500) to Belle, with instructions to pay Lloyd $300 monthly for life, Lloyd scarcely needed the money, being now in receipt of all his stepfather's royalties. In 1896 he had married a schoolteacher from Missouri, Katharine Durham, whom Fanny initially found 'a good, sensible, capable girl, and not too young', a favourable opinion later reversed. The marriage was unhappy and ended in divorce, after which to Fanny's fury, Katharine wrote several books claiming to be 'the truth' about Robert Louis Stevenson. Lloyd wrote several nondescript novels, traded widely on the Stevenson connection, bought expensive cars, took cruises and enjoyed the lifestyle to which he had early become accustomed. An admirer of the Italian fascist Benito Mussolini, he died in the south of France in 1947, aged 79.

Of those who remembered Robert Louis Stevenson, Lloyd's sister Belle was the great survivor. Her inheritance from Louis was land adjacent to Vailima, which she sold when she moved back to the United States. She published *Memories of Vailima* and *This Life I've Loved,* but despite Fanny's legacy, the source of her wealth had little to do with Stevenson. Within months of her mother's death, Belle had married her companion Ned Field; it was the discovery of oil on land belonging to him that made Belle a millionairess. She died in 1957, aged 95.

Postscript

History is much decried; it is a tissue of errors, we are told, no doubt correctly; and rival historians expose each other's blunders with gratification. Yet the worst historian has a clearer view of the period he studies than the best of us can hope to form of that in which we live. The obscurest epoch is today. ...

– 'The Day After Tomorrow', 1887 –

HENRY JAMES, STEVENSON'S most loyal friend and admirer, wrote a tactful letter to Graham Balfour on the publication of *The Life of Robert Louis Stevenson*, congratulating him, but also pointing out that a life story so unusual and adventurous was bound to distract attention from what really mattered, the books the subject had written. This was prophetic, since in the earlier years of the twentieth century interest in the author's life, as manufactured by his widow and stepson and their chosen biographer, was so intense that it threatened to eclipse the work completely. The 'big books' – *Treasure Island*, *Kidnapped* and *Strange Case of Dr Jekyll and Mr Hyde* – retained their popularity with the reading public, but with the rise of Modernism and a change of literary emphasis after the First World War, Stevenson's reputation in academic circles suffered a catastrophic decline. The 'angel clean from heaven' image was derided in a less reverent age, and the biography intended to give it permanency was questioned and discredited.

By the 1920s G. K. Chesterton's was a voice crying in the wilderness; most serious critics disowned Stevenson, accusing him of the affectation of 'fine writing' for its own sake. The kind of poetry he wrote fell out of fashion, and his perceived optimism grated on the sensibility of intellectuals struggling to make sense of a more violent and fractured world. In this atmosphere the word 'Victorian' became a term of abuse, and Stevenson, whose misfortune it had been to die in 1894, was, despite his declared dislike of much nineteenth-century cant and hypocrisy, branded with it. Academic opinion, which might not have mattered much to a general readership, nonetheless had a trickledown effect; school teachers who had been taught by hostile university teachers excluded Stevenson from their syllabuses and much of his work went out of print. He was dropped from serious anthologies of English literature and dismissed as a mere 'children's writer'. Even in Scotland teenagers in the 1950s might have been awarded *The Master of Ballantrae* as a school prize, but they were unlikely to study it as a text in class.

More recently, due principally to a resurgence of interest in Scottish literature within Scotland, the tide has turned in favour of Stevenson. In the later twentieth century a critical re-evaluation led by scholars with Scottish roots – notably Janet Adam Smith, David Daiches and Jenni Calder – brought about a gradual academic rehabilitation. Meanwhile carefully researched biographies – first in the 1950s by J. C. Furnas and most recently by Frank McLynn and Claire Harman – deconstructed the image of Stevenson created by Graham Balfour and which was so at odds with the *zeitgeist* of the modern age. The results of these activities were a more truthful and psychologically penetrating account of an extraordinary life, and a new insight into the way that the life was woven into the writing. There is now an eight-volume edition of *The Collected Letters of Robert Louis Stevenson*, edited by Bradford A. Booth and Ernest Mayhew, which restores the parts of the text which Sidney Colvin, intent on controlling his own and Fanny Sitwell's story, chose to leave out.

It has been said of *Treasure Island* that it was a young man's book, but it equally may be said that all Stevenson's books were a young man's books; he was after all only 44 when he died. What amazes is that in little more than 20 years he produced so much and of such variety – and that between *An Inland Voyage* and *Weir of Hermiston* can be traced such a headlong rush to maturity. Inevitably some of Stevenson's writing, concerned with political and social issues of his own time, is of little interest to modern readers outside universities, but much more is as fresh as the day it was written, infused with his youth and passion and awareness of the ambiguity of human motivation, not least his own. His Calvinist upbringing, his struggle with his father, his marriage, his life in the South Seas, his tumultuous relationships, his love of history and his keen sense of humour, all found their place in the books of a great Scottish writer, whose relevance to a new generation is happily reflected in the greater availability of much of his best work.

Select Bibliography

Publications

AMORETTI, L. N. (2001): *Partage de Mémoire: Ecrivains, artistes, créateurs à Menton* (Menton).

ATKINSON, D. (ed.) (2000): *The Selected Letters of W. E. Henley* (Aldershot).

BALFOUR, G. (1901): *The Life of Robert Louis Stevenson*, 2 volumes (London and New York)

BARNETT, T. RATCLIFFE (n.d.): *Border By-ways and Lothian Lore* (Edinburgh).

BATHURST, B. (1999): The Lighthouse Stevensons (London).

BELL, G. (1849-50, 1973): *Days and Nights in the Wynds of Edinburgh* (Edinburgh).

BINDING, P. (1974): *Robert Louis Stevenson* (London).

BOODLE, A. (1926): *RLS and his Sine Qua Non* (London 1926).

BOOTH, B. A. and MAYHEW, E. (eds) (1995): The Letters of Robert Louis Stevenson, 8 volumes (New Haven and London).

CALDER, J. (1980): *RLS: A Life Study* (London).

CHESTERTON, G. K. (1927): *Robert Louis Stevenson* (London).

COLVIN, S. (ed.) (1921): *The Letters of Robert Louis Stevenson*, volumes 31-35 of the *Tusitala* edition (London).

COLVIN, S. (1924): *Memories and Notes* (London).

CONNELL, J. (1949): *W. E. Henley* (London).

DAICHES, D. (1946): *Robert Louis Stevenson: A Re-evaluation* (London).

DAICHES, D. (1973): *Robert Louis Stevenson and His World* (London).

FERGUSON, DE L. AND WAINGROW, M. (eds) (1956): *Robert Louis Stevenson's Letters to Charles Baxter* (London).

FLANDERS, J. (2003): *The Victorian House* (London).

FURNAS, J. C. (1952): *Voyage to Windward, the Life of Robert Louis Stevenson* (London).

GOSSE, EDMUND (1913): *Critical Kit-kats*.

GRANT, W. (n.d.): *Pentland Ways and Country Days* (London).

GREEN, R. LANCELYN (1946): *Andrew Lang* (Leicester).

HAMILTON, I. (1992): *Keepers of the Flame: Literary Estates and the Rise of Biography* (London).

HARMAN, C. (2005): *Robert Louis Stevenson, A Biography* (London).

HAYTER, A. (1968): *Opium and the Romantic Imagination* (London).

HENLEY W. E. and STEVENSON, R. L. (1874-98): *The Plays of W. E. Henley and Robert Louis Stevenson* (Edinburgh).

HENNESSEY, J. POPE (1974): Robert Louis Stevenson (London).

HOLMES, L. D. (2001): *Treasured Islands* (New York).

HOLMES, R. (1985): *Footsteps: Adventures of a Romantic Biographer* (London).

JAPP, A. H. (1905): *Robert Louis Stevenson* (London).

KNIGHT, A. (1985): *Robert Louis Stevenson Treasury* (London).

KNIGHT, A. (1986): *RLS in the South Seas: An Intimate Photographic Record* (Edinburgh).

LANG, A. (1903): *Adventures Among Books* (London).

LOCHHEAD, M. (1959): *Young Victorians* (London).

MACKAY, M. (1969): *The Violent Friend: The Story of Mrs Robert Louis Stevenson* (London).

McLYNN, F. (1993): *Robert Louis Stevenson* (London).

MASSON, R. (ed.) (1922): *I Can Remember Robert Louis Stevenson* (Edinburgh).

OSBOURNE, L. (1924): *An Intimate Portrait of R.L.S.* (New York).

PICKERING, G. (1974): *Creative Malady* (London).

SANCHEZ, N. V. (1920): *The Life of Mrs Robert Louis Stevenson* (London).

SIMPSON, E. B. (1906): *Robert Louis Stevenson* (Boston and London).

SIMPSON, E. B. (1912): *The R. L. Stevenson Originals* (London).

SKINNER, R. T. (ed.) (1926): *Cummy's Diary: A Diary Kept by Robert Louis Stevenson's Nurse Alison Cunningham While Travelling with him on the Continent During 1863* (London).

SMITH, J. ADAM (1971): *Collected Poems of Robert Louis Stevenson* (London).

STEVENSON, M. I. (1906): *Letters from Samoa 1891-95* (London).

STEVENSON, R. L. (1926): *Collected Works*, Vailima Edition (London).

SWEARINGEN, R. (1986): *The Prose Writings of Robert Louis Stevenson: A Guide* (London).

Works of Robert Louis Stevenson in modern paperback editions:

Poetry, Essays and Letters

A Child's Garden of Verses (Penguin Popular Classics, 2000).
Robert Louis Stevenson: Selected Poems (ed. A. Calder: Penguin Classics, 1998).
The Lantern Bearers and Other Essays (ed. J. Treglown: Cooper Square Press, 1999).
Selected Letters of Robert Louis Stevenson (ed. E. Mehew: Yale Nota Bene, 2001).

Fiction

The Scottish Novels: Kidnapped, Catriona, The Master of Ballantrae and *Weir of Hermiston* (Canongate Classics, 1997).
Treasure Island (Penguin Classics, 2000; and Dollar Academy, 2007).
The Black Arrow (Penguin Classics, 2007).
The Strange Case of Dr Jekyll and Mr Hyde (Penguin Classics, 2006).
The Ebb-tide (Everyman's Classics, 1994).
The Wrecker (with Lloyd Osbourne: Aegypan, 2005).
The Complete Short Stories of Robert Louis Stevenson (ed. B. Menikoff: The Modern Library, 2002).

Travel

Travels with a Donkey in the Cévennes and *The Amateur Emigrant* (Penguin Classics, 2004).
In the South Seas (Penguin Classics, 1988),
South Sea Tales (Oxford World's Classics, 1999).
Dreams of Elsewhere: Selected Travel Writings of Robert Louis Stevenson (ed. J. S. Sawyers: In Pinn, 2004).

Online resources

The National Library of Scotland
    www.nls.uk/rlstevenson/links.html   (accessed April 2008)

Bath University Treasure Island project
    www.ukoln.ac.uk/services/treasure   (accessed April 2008)

The Robert Louis Stevenson Silverado Museum
    www.silveradomuseum.org/   (accessed April 2008)

New and secondhand books by and about Robert Louis Stevenson,
including those listed above:
    www.amazon.co.uk   (accessed April 2008)

Index